LEARNING TO LEAD

By

Willard Claassen

Christian Service Training Series

HERALD PRESS, SCOTTDALE, PENNSYLVANIA

FAITH AND LIFE PRESS, NEWTON, KANSAS

Library of Congress Catalog Card Number: 63-20203
Printed in United States

Foreword

This leadership training unit, *Learning to Lead,* is the first in a series of six ten-week courses on leadership training. One new unit will be published each consecutive year until the series is completed. The titles of other units to follow are: *Learning to Teach, Learning to Understand Pupils, Learning to Know the Bible, Learning to Understand Administration, Learning to Understand the Life and Mission of the Church.* A teacher's guide is published with each unit.

This study of leadership is basic to the entire course. Its purpose is to help teachers and other church workers develop an understanding of leadership in the Christian context. It is hoped that improving leadership functions will help church leaders participate to the fullest extent of their ability in the fellowship and work of the church.

The leader functions within the context of a group. Consequently these studies will involve a rather intensive examination of a leader's relationship to groups. To be an effective leader one should understand what is happening in the group to which he is related.

It may be expected that strongly individualistic persons will react to the emphasis on group life. On the other hand a possible result of these studies may be the development of a more wholesome respect for group life within the church and more respect for and better use of the democratic process to which Mennonites are committed as a way of church government.

A few words of caution may be in order at the outset. Christianity is more than a kind of "togetherness," although that certainly is one aspect. Not all group thinking is effective. When groups are poorly led, badly informed, when they act on the basis of prejudice, or when they are not disposed to act or think responsibly, their efforts to make decisions may be a sheer waste of time. To be able to identify and remedy such situations is one reason for engaging in these studies.

Experience has shown that attempts to be "democratic" in

arriving at group decisions are not effective unless the right conditions prevail. Good group thinking will not occur in a haphazard gabfest, where there is neither plan, procedure, nor information.

Not all group decisions are good decisions. Just as there are individuals who act on impulse, so there are groups that respond too quickly to a suggestion without adequately considering the consequences.

In these studies on leadership we are not discussing ways to manipulate people—to bend their wills to our own wishes! Rather we will try to learn how to improve our relations with other persons and make our relationships with them more Christian. To achieve this goal we will study not only what the Bible says should characterize our relationships to other persons in the brotherhood—love, forbearance, sympathy, forgiveness, and the responsibility for speaking the truth in love. We will also use the findings of social scientists in order to apply these truths to leadership functions.

Teachers and church workers are leaders. Leaders are made, not born. Leadership can be learned. It is hoped that the quality of leadership will be improved as we search for a Christian concept of leadership, and as we learn about the types of leaders and functions of leaders. We will discuss the characteristics of immature and mature groups, what is involved in the process of communication, the roles of group members, creating an atmosphere for redemptive activity, how to make decisions, and how to set goals and evaluate results.

It is not impossible that members of the family will find that the stimulation in these studies will make family relationships more Christlike.

The outlines for these six courses in the Christian Service Training Series have been prepared jointly by the Mennonite Board of Education and Publication, Newton, Kans., and the Mennonite Commission for Christian Education, Scottdale, Pa.

Contents

Chapter 1

The Need for Leaders

Our world seems to be stumbling through one crisis into another. Whole continents—such as Africa for example—are in ferment. Accepted ways of doing things are being challenged. If our church is to minister to a world in revolution, Christian leaders must be found and prepared who not only know the message of the Gospel, but know how to relate it with love, patience, and understanding to the people caught in the turmoil and tensions of our generation.

While there are a few hermits—people haters who cut themselves off from all human associations—most of us relate to groups of people. We live in groups, we work in groups, we play in groups, we plan in groups, we learn in groups, we visit in groups, we worship in groups.

It is not surprising then that much of our work in the church is group-centered. The congregation itself is a group. Within the congregation are Sunday-school classes for all ages, teachers for these classes, teachers' classes, men's brotherhoods, mission societies, youth fellowships, boys' clubs, girls' clubs, midweek classes, special study groups, choirs, committees, and church councils.

If these groups are to function effectively, capable Christian leaders must be found. The preacher cannot carry the whole load on his shoulders. There must be available a core of Christian leaders adequately prepared to function in positions of leadership.

That's what this manual is about. In these studies we will try to gain new insights into what is involved in "learning to lead."

As a church worker you may see yourself as a leader. Perhaps you are a teacher, a committee chairman, or the leader of a boys' club. Your performance as a leader is influenced to considerable extent by your idea of what a leader is. Before you commit yourself to any one kind of leadership, let's see whether we can get some additional insight into the leadership process.

There is a saying that some are born to leadership, some achieve leadership, and others have leadership thrust upon them. In the work of the church, elections being what they are, those who have leadership thrust upon them for the first time often feel frustrated and baffled by this new responsibility. Perhaps some of the perplexity about what to do as a leader arises from prevalent conflicting ideas about leadership.

Theories of Leadership

Leadership is a difficult term to define because it means so many different things to different people. There are various styles and philosophies of leadership. Some think of leadership in terms of power or authority, some as personality traits, still others as status or position.

Let's examine some theories of leadership.

1. There is the *great man theory* of leadership. According to this view, the leader possesses uncommon talents or abilities. Leadership qualities are said to be the product of personality traits. The idea often crops up that leaders tend to be taller, heavier, and more energetic than nonleaders. While it is possible that tall, energetic people may impress others more than short, slight, or sluggish individuals, it is nevertheless true that many world-famous leaders had none of these characteristics. From what we know about the Apostle Paul, he did not have a commanding physical presence.

Intelligence, initiative, and self-confidence have also been singled out and related to leadership in numerous studies. It would be shortsighted to deny the influence of these characteristics on leadership, but that argument can be pushed too far. It should be encouraging to many of us to learn that there is evidence to support the position that persons of exceptional intelligence are less likely to be found in positions of leadership than individuals who are not sharply set off from their fellows by intelligence.

Some call attention to the personality trait of dominance in leadership. According to this view a leader is a person who can dominate the group. Those who have studied leadership under laboratory conditions have observed that more often than not the proffered leadership of dominating persons is rejected. As we shall see later on, the Christian leader is the one who is least inclined to act as the "boss," or to pose as the "expert" who knows all the answers, or who acts as the person who feels he must run the group.

2. Another theory of leadership is that it is the result of being in a situation or office of leadership. Proponents of this theory hold that a leader can emerge only if the times are right to permit him to use whatever skills and ambitions he might possess. Advocates of this theory like to point out that had Edison or Ford lived in the seventeenth century they could not have invented the phonograph or the Ford car. While there are elements of truth here, the theory has the fatal weakness that it imputes to environment a power it does not possess.

3. Again leadership is said to be the result of a certain style of relationship to groups. According to this theory a leader is that individual who is regarded by the members of his group as having "influence" over them, and is chosen by them more often than other members. One wonders whether this theory does not find wide acceptance in the church today. Who is elected teacher, the person who has actual ability or the person that has "influence"? This theory has the weakness of being a static interpretation of leadership. It is based on the idea of status. The leader is chosen because of traits that call attention to himself. However, being chosen for a *position* of leadership does not necessarily result in leadership *behavior* on the part of the person elected. He may merely be a headman. Headmanship is not synonymous with leadership.

Margaret E. Kuhn says, "Some people in the churches confuse headship and leadership. Formal leaders are elected or appointed to have some authority in the church's work, may not be persons who have the greatest influence in the groups they serve. They may be admired and respected but their headship may not give them leadership, as we have been considering leadership.

"Leadership as distinguished from headship, therefore, is determined not only by the problem before the group, and the needs of the members, but by the spirit in which an individual has related himself to other people and is able to draw out their suggestions, opinions, feelings, and guide others toward the achievement of their individual and group goals and toward the constructive solutions of their problems. Heads of groups become recognized leaders of groups as they are able to help group members to feel greater satisfaction in the group and to move toward the fulfillment of their needs and objectives."[1]

We have been saying that many persons are looked upon as leaders because they have position, rank, wealth, power, or authority, or because they have reputation, skill, and knowledge, or personality and glamor. These qualities are too often superficially associated with leadership. While they may be real factors in the situation, they do not provide satisfactory explanations for a Christian concept of leadership.

4. Consequently leadership is thought by others to be a set of functions. This concept will be developed in the next section.

What Does a Leader Do?

If leadership is inadequately defined in the qualities mentioned above, then what is it? Rather than to ask, "What kind of a person makes a good leader?" researchers have more recently been asking, "What does an effective leader do?"

Recent studies in leadership indicate that leadership may be thought of as a set of functions rather than the traditional definition of position or personality traits. This emphasizes the concept that leaders are made not born. If leadership is a set of functions, we can learn them. In the Christian brotherhood everyone may become a leader in the sense that in given situations his abilities and resources may be used to further the progress of the group.

Leadership is taking responsibilities and performing certain functions in relationship with other persons to advance a group or organization toward its objectives.

This definition of leadership makes clear at least three concepts: (1) If leadership is the performance of certain functions that advance the goal of the group, it is not the same thing as holding office. Consequently any member who acts responsibly to advance the group toward its goal is involved in a leadership role as surely as officeholders. (2) Leadership is identified in terms of the relationship a person has with other people and his ability to help a group use its resources to solve problems. This kind of a leader is not a "lone wolf" but rather a participating member of a community. He remains humble and sensitive to the needs of others. (3) Those functions that do not help to carry out the purposes for which the group exists but which, though well intentioned, deter, delay, and obstruct the objectives of the group, do not constitute leadership.

Three-Dimensional Training for Leadership

Leadership training is therefore not the simple undertaking it was once thought to be. Malcolm Knowles[2] points out that to develop competent leaders we now have to work in three dimensions.

The first is the one we would think of first: training for particular skills such as being chairman of a committee, leading a discussion, presiding at a meeting, or teaching a certain subject.

The second dimension in leadership training is learning to understand group life. This second dimension may be compared to the "liberal arts" element in leadership training, whereas the first is more like "vocational training."

The third dimension consists of training all members of a group, not just the designated leaders, to perform leadership functions. This is why all of us should learn how to lead. *The second and third dimensions will be discussed in this manual.*

Who Is a Leader?

Leadership is not a mystic quality that some persons possess and others do not. Leadership may be learned. Leadership is what a person does for the group. The leader is a person who can move a group to act. The group has power to change or to withhold leadership, depending on what it wishes to do. One of the factors that determines whether a group will confer leadership is the prospective leader's ability to achieve in an area which has prestige for the group.

For example, small children tend to make no distinction between a hero and a leader. What makes a hero for children or for youth is sometimes baffling to adults. In one first-grade class the hero, and by implication the leader, was the boy who could spit the farthest. Among teen-agers the physically well coordinated boy skilled in sports easily becomes the hero-leader.

Adults, too, may be confused about who is the leader. Popularity is often confused with leadership. In school the most popular person may be the class clown. Yet the group may not be moved to action by him. Among adults the most chosen person may not be the one who really succeeds in getting harmony and action from a group.

As groups become more mature, they increase in their ability to distinguish between popularity and leadership. Much could be said about elections of leaders and administrators in Sunday schools and other church organizations in this connection. How mature are Christians in selecting leaders for the work of the church? Popularity is not necessarily leadership, but popularity wins elections.

Designated and Undesignated Leaders

In addition to asking what leadership is, we need to make some additional distinctions about leadership functions.

Leadership was defined as a set of functions that advance the group toward its goal. In a mature group everyone can perform leadership functions if he has the necessary resources to make a contribution. In a group there are two kinds of leaders—the designated, or appointed leader, and members who act as leaders by performing leadership roles. The latter are called undesignated leaders. Seen in this way, the designated leader may not always be the real leader of the group; the real leader is any person who has the good sense to make a proposal that helps the group solve its problem. A new set of circumstances—perhaps a crisis, a stalemate, a need for specialized information, the need for tact or humor—may call for leadership roles from undesignated leaders.

In a Christian group each member has the responsibility of accepting leadership roles whenever the group can use his contribution. As members seek to discover what contribution is needed, they should be open to the guidance of the Holy Spirit.

Leadership in the Bible

Is there something about a Christian leader that sets him off as different from other leaders? We must admit with considerable embarrassment that we often observe little difference between Christian and secular leaders. Some church groups are dull and apathetic, with little concern shown among members largely because of the poor leadership being given. Some group are led by despots who make no pretense about who is boss. Under their leadership group members build up resentment and hostility.

Perhaps you have observed in a church meeting or a committee the kind of situation described here: "I wanted my church to be able to move and so I took an aggressive position and I pushed the matter through, but some people were ridden over in the process. I wonder if I desired most the welfare of my church. . . .

"I wanted to do what is right, but I can't do what I ought to do. Perhaps it is my pride and my desire to put my own self before everything else. That is the highest hurdle to my usefulness. Dare I understand the deeper layers of *me* enough to get my pride and selfishness out of the way for *me* to be useful."[3]

Does the Bible teach anything about leadership? We believe it does. All the Scriptures that have a bearing on our relationship to other people apply to leadership. Because such passages are so numerous only typical references can be alluded to here. In addition to the passages themselves, we have the example of early church leaders in the New Testament.

The following Scriptures speak to the point, "And be ye kind one to another, tenderhearted, forgiving one another, even as God for Christ's sake hath forgiven you" (Ephesians 4:32). Dietrich Bonhoeffer reminds us, "Christian brotherhood is not an ideal which we must realize; it is rather a reality created by God in Christ in which we may participate."[4] Paul's counsel to the Philippians is pertinent. "Let nothing be done through strife or vainglory; but in lowliness of mind let each esteem other better than themselves. Look not every man on his own things, but every man also on the things of others. Let this mind be in you, which was also in Christ Jesus" (Philippians 2:3-5).

Or, "What credit is it, if when you do wrong and are beaten for it you take it patiently? But if when you do right and suffer for it you take it patiently, you have God's approval" (I Peter 2:20). Applying this to the challenge of Christian leadership, Jesse H. Ziegler observes, "Each of us has received much we neither deserved nor earned. A mother's love nurtured us from the beginning. We did nothing to earn it. She was able to give love because she was the recipient of love. Many of us received the affection of other mature people who gave us what they would like to have given to children of their own. These times of receiving love that was unearned, undeserved, sometimes almost accidental helped to form us.

"But to live as mature members of our culture we must be prepared to receive other emotions that are undeserved and of which we may be the almost accidental target. Hostility and resentment must have a target. If my friend or neighbor is prevented by internal or external prohibitions from expressing these feelings toward the person who stimulates them, I may suffer unjustly.

"Can I take it patiently? Can we have insight enough and grace enough to absorb some of the ill that needs to be absorbed, as well as the love that has formed us? This in reality is required of the mature person. This is what God approves."[5]

There will be not a few occasions when the leader who seeks to draw out timid members or attempts to work out a compromise between opposing viewpoints will draw hostility upon himself. Occasionally a group unable to carry through a task takes out its frustrations on the leader. Sometimes he will be blamed for not telling them what to do, when in reality they may not want to carry out the task.

Franklin H. Littell reminds us that the early Anabaptists made much of the application of the principle of consensus as a channel through which the Holy Spirit made His will known to the brotherhood. There is a startling phrase used to sum up the Jerusalem conference recorded in Acts 15:28, "For it seemed good to the Holy Ghost, *and to us,* to lay upon you no greater burden than these necessary things. . . ." Though we might have expected them to do so, neither Peter, Paul, nor James laid the decision on the line. Rather they sought consensus under the guidance of the Holy Spirit. This is a good Scriptural description of the leader's function.

The Leader's Motivation

When we think about leadership from the Christian perspective, we must reckon with the fact that there are many motivations to leadership which are less than Christian. Why does the leader want to lead? Is he driven by the desire to dominate others? Is power his goal? Is it for prestige or for status? Is it the desire to be popular? Or does it have something to do with swelling one's bank account as is frequently the case in politics.

The leader needs to examine his philosophy of leadership. The mature Christian leader is subject to Christ as his Leader. He receives his leadership as a trust while he exercises leadership roles. He is led by Christ.

This leader has actually nothing to give that has not been given. His willingness to lead is born of the desire to serve. He realizes that as a child of God he can be a vehicle through which the saving love of God can be communicated to others.

He sees his relation to the group as an opportunity to share the love of Christ. He does not see the group as something to manipulate but encourages persons to explore the freedom that is in Christ. With the security he finds in Christ he can accept both praise and blame without becoming angry. He knows that the burden of leadership is not carried alone, but is shared with Him who said, "Lo, I am with you alway."

Chapter 2

Leaders and How They Work

A person tends to be like the people with whom he lives and works. Not altogether, but to a remarkable extent the atmosphere and structure of a group can control the behavior of individual members. And the group as a whole tends to take on qualities communicated by its designated leader.

An experiment conducted by Lewin, Lippitt, and White showed how this works. The same group of children was found to be easy to deal with under one leader but aggressive and unruly under another. At the same time, children shifted from one group to another tended to conform to the atmosphere of the the new group.[1] Thus the attitude and function of the designated leader need our attention.

Types of Leadership

For purposes of discussion at least four types of leaders will be identified. Some writers identify more types than this.

The *autocratic leader* is one who likes to dominate people. He makes plans for the group himself. In his relationship to the group, he stresses the importance of discipline. His deference to authority is obvious. He lays down the law expecting the group to follow. He makes decisions without "wasting time" in counseling with his group. He relies not on persuasion or group consensus but on the powers inherent in his office. Or he secures action by threat or punishment. He considers the alternatives and reserves to himself the prerogative of decision-making.

Have you seen this leader somewhere in a committee or a church group? Mr. A was a lay leader in one congregation. He had a strong voice and equally strong convictions about the way things should be done in the church. He could get up and present his ideas forcefully and persuasively enough to persuade a majority to accept his position, thus overriding the objections of the minority who could not accept them. For a time the minority was defeated and building up defiance. Finally after another such defeat, the minority took drastic and unpleasant steps to make sure their viewpoint would be heard and understood by the congregation.

You may have encountered the autocratic leader as a chairman of a committee. He had asked some of the members beforehand to present his viewpoint. The discussion seemed to be stacked. It was not free and open. He didn't trust the members, and at the first opportunity called for a vote to end the discussion.

It will surprise no one that autocratic leaders are found in churches. What happens to members of a group under this kind of leadership? When members of a group discover their ideas are not wanted or not listened to, they stop giving them. If no one is going to pay attention, why bother to express ideas. Then people begin to resent the leader who makes it impossible for them to participate. When this kind of leadership is found in the church, the results are frequently disastrous to Christian fellowship. Resentment toward the leader may lead people to break away from the fellowship of the church and feel great bitterness toward it. Those members who do remain under the influence of an autocratic leader frequently become dependent and unresourceful.

In some ways the opposite of the autocratic leadership is the *laissez-faire type* of leadership. Under this kind of leadership the group does pretty much as it pleases. This interpretation of leadership sees the leader reflecting the thoughts of the members and maintaining the unity of the group. This leader's behavior is basically nonevaluative. He might be dubbed the "do-nothing leader." Such a leader may imagine he is using the democratic process, but actually he is misusing it.

What happens to people when the laissez-faire type is in the chair? One of the most apparent results is apathy. There are frequent yawns because the leader has not bothered to identify the real problems confronting the group; discussions seem unimportant or they are off the beam. Few persons participate. Members come late or do not show up at all. There are overquick decisions and failure to follow through on decisions. There is reluctance to assume responsibility and failure to make plans for the next meeting.

Researchers have discovered another leader type that falls somewhere between the autocratic and the democratic type. They refer to this one as the *benevolent autocrat* type. This leader has been characterized as "the overseer" who solicitously cares for the group. While he is an autocratic leader at heart, his personal designs are benevolent. It's just that he knows what is best for people and he aims to see that his will is done because as the saying goes, "Father knows best."

What happens to the members of the group under this kind of leadership? Members tend to become timid, complacent, unresourceful, and unimaginative; they seem unable to get out of a rut because they are always looking to the leader for the answers. If the leader knows the answers, why bother to find new ones?

The characteristics of the *democratic* leader stand off sharply from these other types. This kind of leader is not primarily interested in the possession of power over others but in stimulating members to participate in group activities and decisions. He relies on persuasion and conciliation rather than on force. He has tolerance for human weakness. His relation to members is cordial and friendly rather than distant and authoritarian. He tends to trust people's good sense. His followers do not put him on a pedestal but tend to see in him only a common man like themselves. This kind of a leader has been called a "catalyst" in the sense that he encourages members of the group to participate and to react.

With democratic leadership, members of a group develop initiative in taking responsibility. They grow in group productivity, and they follow through on decisions because they participated in making them.

In writing about the types of leadership, Gordon Lippitt illustrated them by referring to youth leaders he knew while helping in YMCA work.

"In leading a group of younger boys into a game of basketball, the *autocratic* type had all the youngsters following him in a line from a locker room to the gym floor. He told every boy which team he was on and which position he was to play. The autocratic leader then picked the two captains, named himself referee, and blew his whistle at every opportunity to assert his authority.

"The *laissez-faire* type just said, 'Hi,' to his boys, grabbed a basketball and his chemistry textbook, and then headed for the gym. When the boys had all arrived on the gym floor, he simply rolled the ball out from the side lines, said, 'Go to it,' leaned back against the wall, and buried his face in his book.

"The *democratic* type called his boys together in the locker room and participated as a member of the group while the group decided what the composition of the two teams was to be and who were to be the captains. He didn't boss them. He gave them advice and guidance. Then he followed them up to the gym floor and got the game under way with as little interference from himself as possible."[2]

Following are contrasts in autocratic and democratic types of leadership:

Autocratic Leadership	*Democratic Leadership*
gives orders	makes suggestions asks questions
gets compliance regardless of consent or agreement	works for willing co-operation, gets consent and agreement
demands and pushes people	*leads* and *persuades*
one-man rule	utilizes the group
autocrat says go	democratic leader says come
depends on external authority	depends on internal motivation
autocratic leader generates resistance	democratic leader generates co-operation

Functions of the Designated Leader

In the discussion about leadership in the last chapter, a distinction was made between designated and undesignated leaders. There we tried to identify the concept of "shared leadership." If leadership is a set of functions which initiate or forward the action of a group toward its goal, then any member of the group can take leadership roles if he has the necessary resources to make a contribution.

In the context of the work of the church, the designated leader may be the teacher of a Sunday-school class. He may be the superintendent of the Sunday school or the chairman of the Christian education committee. The teacher may be elected by the class. Sometimes teachers are appointed. The chairman of the committee may have volunteered for the job. As pointed out previously, the designated leader may not always be the real leader of the group. Sometimes it may be an ordinary member of the group who is able to help rally the members and enable them to accomplish their task.

Good functioning groups need various functions, such as the giving of specialized information, release of tension, clarification, summarization of progress made, and reconciliation. Depending upon the circumstance, various members of the group emerge as leaders as they possess resources to meet these needs.

In a Christian group each member has the responsibility of helping the group to achieve its goal. He remains alert to opportunities to contribute leadership where needed. He is able to curb his own needs and personal wishes when necessary to let others lead.

Administrators in the Sunday school, teachers, or chairmen of committees and other church workers are constantly called upon to act as designated leaders. Perhaps the functions of designated or appointed leader in a church group can be seen more clearly by looking at the experience of a leader of a class of junior highs.

It was October and Harold had just started a new Sunday-school class of junior highs. From his relation to the members of his class we may see more clearly the functions of a designated leader. Harold didn't really know the members of his class. There were ten pupils. He didn't even know their names, much less what the names stood for. Later on the name Richard would bring a vivid image to his mind, but today he was a blank stranger. Some of the pupils came from rural homes, most of them from the city. Some of their parents were active workers in the church. Their average age was thirteen years. They were full of energy.

There was Richard who showed signs of not wanting to cooperate in the first class session. Allen was quiet and unresponsive. Russell seemed especially nervous. Lois was shy. Judy was talkative and responded on nearly everything.

Harold tried to take it all in. It was really more than he could take in during one session. He knew he must try to know his pupils and try to understand them before he could help them. Here we identify one of the functions of designated leadership: *to learn to know and understand persons in the group.*

But Harold did something else the first session. He took a friendly interest in the members of his class. He tried to get next to them. To Allen's hesitancy he responded with warmth and support. To Richard he listened quietly. He helped Lois make some new friends. He gave Judy opportunities to take responsibility.

Here we identify the importance of *the designated leader's role in establishing a good climate in the group.* How the leader performs this function will determine whether the atmosphere in the group is characterized by feelings of hostility (often unspoken), criticism, and threat; or his attitude will help the group build mutual confidence and a free-working relationship, based on understanding, acceptance, and friendship. Members of the group should feel free to express their ideas and feel comfortable and at home in the group.

Then Harold took stock of the new classroom. There was a table. Substantial, well-arranged chairs encouraged order. He discovered that singing helped the group settle down. Some pupils responded better when they stayed seated than when standing. He decided that Richard and Russell should not sit together. These observations illustrate another aspect of the appointed leader's role—that of *creating an atmosphere in which members can be free and comfortable.*

Harold studied what he had learned about his group. He thought about what it ought to do. There were the goals he thought he should help his group attain. One was "to help the youngsters have a good time discussing their problems in class." Another was "to help them learn to work together in planning a worship service." He had some individual goals too: "help Richard cut the 'yackety-yack' and help him to see some relationship between talk and conduct." There were Bible lessons to teach.

This identifies another function of the designated leader. Harold was thinking about ways *to help his group determine goals and objectives.* While he knew where he wanted to go, he was at the same time aware that the members of his class might not be ready to do what he wanted to do. In other words, he was trying to determine how he could secure the co-operation of his class to share these goals. He was also trying to see clearly what he personally was trying to accomplish.

Harold's class was one of the liveliest in the school. It had been a challenge to discover the interests of his pupils and then to build on these interests in a vital and spiritual way. He noticed the junior highs' interest in sports—their never-ending energy. Sometimes they almost wore him out in a half hour. He noticed that if they were grouped properly, they liked to work together. He noticed also a worship service they had planned was unusually effective. Some were beginning to build habits of private worship. Their sense of justice and fairness was keen. How could he latch on to these interests?

In this case Harold was trying *to identify the resources of his group.* How could he use the resources of the group toward achieving common objectives? How could he help the group organize itself to work most effectively?

But Harold also wondered why members of his class didn't respond the way they should. Why did Allen withdraw? What was the matter with Richard? He was a rebel. Why did Russell "freeze up"? and what would it take to "thaw him out"? How could he keep Judy from monopolizing the discussion?

He tried putting members of his group in smaller committees to work out problems. He tried to draw out each member of the group in participation so that he might have an opportunity for growth. He tried to establish a relationship of understanding and love among the members of his group.

This identifies another function of the designated leader, that of *helping members of the group to participate in meaningful ways.*

One Sunday Harold discovered that he could not begin to cover the Bible lesson assigned for that Sunday. His class didn't seem to be interested in staying with the lesson. Talkative Judy insisted on telling the class about her older sister who got a job in a distant city. Then Richard, who liked to talk himself, got into an argument with Judy. Harold noticed there were some other things that needed straightening out before he could get on with the lesson.

In this experience Harold learned that "individual needs" must be taken care of before the group tasks can be completed. In his case the task was teaching the lesson. This identifies *the designated leader's responsibility for being sensitive to the individual member's needs, and maintaining a balance between task functions and group maintenance.*

Harold got into the habit of reflecting on his class experiences. At first it was pretty hard to recall what had really happened. Sometimes there was so much he couldn't remember it all. But after disciplining himself, he got so he could spot certain crucial things. He began asking questions like these: Why did I do that? Did this procedure hinder or help the group today? Did I allow the members of my class to develop individual motivation? Did I make it possible for them to tell me what they really wanted to tell me? Did I make sufficient allowance for members of the class to make their contributions on their level of understanding? How could I have provided better leadership?

In this way Harold was fulfilling *the designated leader's role of evaluating the progress of the group.*

Summary

The designated leader's function is to aid growth, not to

force it. It is therefore important that we see the leadership functions that can improve our work with groups. They are summarized as follows:

1. It is the designated leader's function to work with the group rather than to do things for it. His influence is indirect rather than direct.

2. He helps the group decide clearly what its purposes and goals are. It is particularly important at the beginning of the group's life that it have a clear understanding of the goals it wants to reach. It may require time and patience on the leader's part until individual goals are integrated with the group's goals. The Christian leader has the added responsibility of understanding the purpose of the Christian fellowship and to communicate this purpose. One of these purposes may be to realize within the experience of a small group what redemptive fellowship is.

3. The designated leader helps the group discover its resources by leading it to become aware of talents, skills, and other resources within its membership.

4. The designated leader assists the group in developing organization needed to carry on its work. He helps the group adopt standards of performance and of conduct.

5. The leader helps the group to accept new ideas and new members with a minimum of conflict. (When conflict develops, he helps the group use it to accomplish something.) He helps the group improve self-discipline in working toward long-range objectives. In the work of the church this may mean helping the group understand other groups which differ from it and aid the group in developing co-operative intergroup relationships.

6. The designated leader will help the group determine its procedures. For example, he will need to guide the group in the various steps of decision-making. (The process of decision-making will be discussed in session 8.)

7. The designated leader must be conscious at all times of the relation between the task (what the group is supposed to be doing) and maintenance (keeping members happy and relationships in order). He will see to it that task function and group maintenance functions are kept in balance. He will exercise his leadership

functions to help a group avoid riding rough shod over members' personal "needs" in order to accomplish a task.

8. The leader helps the group evaluate its progress and its capacity and limitations. If a group is to learn to work effectively, it must be willing to analyze the causes for its failures. For example, the group a writer was in had recorded a favorable response on an action in a previous meeting. The topic came up for discussion in a later meeting. After more discussion on the same topic in which two members of the group who had previously been absent also participated, a member of the group did not support the proposed action. There was a long pause; no one picked up the idea. This group began to think about what had happened. One member helped the group by saying rather bluntly, "Some people here are not saying what they really think. In the last meeting you were for the idea, tonight you are not." This helped the group face what was rather obviously true and to proceed from that point.

1. Keith Davis and William G. Scott, editors, *Readings in Human Relations* (New York: McGraw-Hill Book Company, Inc., 1959), p. 223.

2. Gordon L. Lippitt, "How to Get Results from a Group," reprinted from *Office Executive,* January 1955, p. 15.

Chapter 3

When a Group Is Immature

In the past 15 years the term "group dynamics" has appeared more and more often in the literature of Christian education. The expression has often been misunderstood; sometimes it has been misused. It is misused, for example, when people say they are going to practice "group dynamic techniques." The term "group dynamics" comes from an area of research in the social sciences known as the study of the "dynamics of groups." The dynamics of the group describe the forces in the group which influence the behavior of group members. It is therefore improper to say that one uses group dynamic techniques. It would be more proper to observe that in a group a member is subject to the influence of group dynamics.

When one analyzes the dynamics in a group, he asks, for example, What are the motivations of the members? What are the real reasons as over against the stated reasons for being members of a group? Do the members accept each other wholeheartedly or are there underlying animosities which crop up in subtle ways? Do the members have difficulty understanding each other? Do they keep discussion on the track? Are there status problems in the group? Do the members speak as freely when certain members of the group are present? Does the group have clear purposes or goals? Or, are they drifting without a rudder?

These and many other questions can be asked about the way

groups function. As persons who work with groups in the church, the question for us is, How can a better understanding of the dynamics of groups help us be better teachers or church workers?

We Work in Groups

We all belong to groups. When you stop to think of it, we belong to quite a large number of groups—family groups, work groups, church groups, recreation groups, school groups. In each of these groups there are forces at work—easy to feel, but hard to pin down—that determine what members do and what the entire group does.

Group dynamics experts say that each individual group has a distinct personality and life of its own shaped by the way members feel about the group and about their specific reasons for joining the group. This is why groups may be characterized as being immature or mature.

In this booklet we will postpone until later a discussion of ways of looking at groups to consider some practical aspects of our relationship to groups. Who has not come home from a committee meeting feeling something was wrong? What happened in the meeting that didn't meet our expectations? Why didn't Susan Loud let anyone else get a word in edgewise? Why did each member of the building committee have a different idea of what the committee ought to do? Why couldn't the committee come to a decision?

What Immature Groups Are Like

What are the characteristics of an immature group? The atmosphere is stiff and formal. People address each other as Mr. or Mrs. or Dr. Individuals tend to be judged by wealth, clothes, degrees, or status in other groups. Members do not listen to each other very well. They are so busy thinking of what they want to say next that they don't listen to others. Members are afraid of controversial issues. They fear conflict because it might split the group. There is a certain amount of hypocrisy present because members fear expressions of hostility and are overly polite to one another when they really do not "feel polite."

The group seems to be unaware of the personal needs of members and rides rough shod over them to accomplish its task. Members tend to perform only one role, such as favoring everything or opposing everything. The matter of guiding the group is left entirely to the designated leader, who receives all credit for success and all blame for failure. Compromise is regarded as undesirable. Individuals tend to reject and develop hostility toward those who disagree with them. The characteristics listed above are symptoms of a "sick" group.

What ways can be discovered to help groups function more adequately? There are clues that all is not going well with the group. Can we make sense out of these clues?

Handling Ambiguity and Confusion

Two of the biggest blocks to good group relationships are unresolved ambiguity and confusion. Usually each member of the group works in ways consistent with his understanding of such a situation to reduce the confusion. Some look for structure in such circumstances by fighting. Others try aggressive behavior or feel out where the boundaries are. What can we do in this group? What can't we do? Experienced teachers recall this kind of behavior in the classroom with children in the early sessions of a new class.

Members of the class aren't sure of their relationship to the new designated leader so they test out how far they can go. They may talk, throw erasers or spitballs, or argue to find out where the boundaries are. Others refuse to accept the problem of confusion at all and withdraw. Still others pair off with a partner either during or after the meeting to try to build up enough confidence to express their feelings to the whole group. Others look desperately to the leader to reduce their confusion.

The leader's challenge is to recognize that members work in different ways to reduce confusion and that it is his responsibility to make positive and constructive use of these individual efforts to solve a problem. The leader must help clarify the group goal in such a way that some aspect of what each individual is doing contributes to the group goal. It will help him to understand that sometimes an individual is meeting his own needs and at other times he contributes to the needs of the group. (These task and maintenance functions of group members will be discussed in more detail later.)

The leader and members of the group need to become sensitive to symptoms of insecurity, and learn how to deal with these problems in a helpful way.

Wrong Persons in a Group

Sometimes the wrong combination of persons in a group makes it difficult for the group to function. For example, a power struggle between several members of the group may keep it from accomplishing anything constructive. The presence of an authority figure in the group may frighten other members of the group so that they do not function properly. This is an admission that sometimes a group may be so constituted that it becomes practically impossible to do its work.

Writing about this problem, Lawrence K. Frank says, "But first it must be recognized that we cannot assume that everyone is rational and capable of listening and learning from discussion. Unfortunately, there are some persons who, though they are not 'crazy or insane,' are very rigid personalities and cannot tolerate anyone who differs from their ideas, especially in certain areas or topics. Moreover, there are some individuals with very strong beliefs and emotionally toned convictions which they want to express repeatedly. There are also some personalities who have developed chronic feelings of anxiety and who must have certainty at all costs. They are upset if they hear anyone voicing different opinions. Then, too, there are some personalities who are chronically hostile, feeling strong resentment toward the world and expressing their hostility to people without any justification. These persons react against anyone because they are 'spoiling for a fight.' "[1]

On the other hand, this should not be taken as license to abandon a group merely because the going is rough. All groups have problems to overcome; conflicting ideas and opinions are normal in every group. All groups are capable of learning to work more effectively. New groups are generally immature because they have not learned to work together, how to understand each other, or how to handle problem situations. A collection of able people does not necessarily make an able committee.

"A collection of mature adults may form a very immature group. Once a group is assembled it assumes a character and existence all its own. It may grow into maturity or it may remain infantile. It may become productive or stay impotent. It may develop weaknesses. It may never build the necessary group strength to withstand the sudden shock of too much conflict or an avalanche of new members . . . finally a group may die before its time; or it may grow senile and useless, and yet continue to exist and thus block the formation of a necessary new group."[2]

Four Common Problems

For purposes of this study, we single out four common problems of immature groups, and suggest ways of dealing with these situations. These problems are: conflict (sometimes developing into hostility), apathy (competent people won't talk), indecision (cannot decide on what to do), and hidden agendas (real concerns are under the surface).

1. *Conflict.* In any group situation the expression of conflicting ideas is normal. The unmistakable signs of conflict are: disagreement leading to argumentation, nasty cracks, subtle remarks with double meaning intended to deflate someone, a tense atmosphere, an open conflict.

Perhaps an actual experience in a committee will make this clearer. Bill was in a planning committee for workers in Christian education. One of the members of the group was a seminary professor. Other members of the group were not teachers but had similar experiences and abilities. Rather unconsciously, the professor took the leadership role, as if there were a class of seminary students around him. The group became more and more tense as the hour dragged on. Members of the group resented being treated like students. Finally one of the members said to the professor, "Dick, if you would keep quiet, and not treat this group like little children, perhaps we could make more progress." This brought the conflict out into the open so that it could be dealt with. But in many situations the member may not have the courage this person had to face a self-styled authority figure or open conflict. Instead tensions and hostilities develop.

Conflict may be expressed in many ways. Members become impatient with each other. Ideas are attacked even before they are completely presented or they are not listened to carefully when they are presented. Members take sides and refuse to compromise. Members attack each other on the personal level. Thinking is strongly colored by emotion. Members distort or get only fragments of the other members' contributions (don't listen). They may disagree with the leader's suggestions, accuse each other of not understanding the real point, or blame the group for lack of progress.

Members of groups within the church may get bogged down by sharp difference of opinion expressed in groups. However, we should remember that we can learn through conflicting points of view. Properly handled, they stimulate discussion. Where all attitudes are similar, prevailing attitudes and prejudices are strengthened by the group. Without challenge, people may become complacent and be overconfident that they have solved all their problems correctly. Under such circumstances no real learning takes place. Sometimes a strong interchange of opinions shakes people out of their bias and mind-set. Social scientists say that it is easier to change the opinions and conduct of persons in a group than it is to change an individual's opinion and conduct when he is isolated from a group.

In Mennonite Church groups, particularly, we often tend to aim for the avoidance of conflict at all costs. This is especially true on the floor of conference sessions. We tend to believe that agreement is absolutely necessary to hold a group together, without really understanding that group cohesiveness is not so much a matter of everybody agreeing as it is a healthy interaction among group members with differing viewpoints, capabilities, and roles. So Christian groups avoid stimulating encounter in conflicting ideas for the sake of "unity." This may be one reason why church groups go stale.

It may be helpful to point out a variety of situations that tend to get groups into fighting moods.

(1) Conflict may occur when a group is given an impossible task and members feel they are unable to meet the demands made of them. The likelihood of conflict is increased when the group is related to a larger organization, as small church groups frequently are. Perhaps the job is too big, or the committee is too small. Possibly the committee was not given a clear assignment (ambiguity again).

(2) Conflict may develop when members fight for status in the group. The job the committee is working on is used as a pretext for jockeying for power, trying to deflate and reduce the prestige of certain members, or establishing cliques. Attack may be aimed at the leader, in which case his suggestions are not followed.

(3) Members may have loyalties outside the group. As individuals coming into a group, we are subject to many influences. Writers on group relations frequently refer to an "invisible committee" standing behind each individual member of the group, influencing his thinking and conduct.

When members of a committee represent an outside organization, what the committee wants to accomplish may conflict with the members' loyalty to the outside organization. For example, a local church building committee may be setting up a schedule for a financial campaign from April to June. One of the building committee members is also a member of a college board of directors. He knows his institution is also planning a campaign at the same time and it needs money desperately. He feels that the church's building campaign will undercut the college's efforts, so he wants to block or radically change the building committee's plans. He feels the educational institution had this scheduled a long time ago and that the local building committee should not disrupt this plan. But he does not have the courage to say this openly, so he merely tries to block the building committee's plans.

Good leadership is the first requisite for handling conflict creatively. Writing about the functions of leadership in handling conflict creatively, Margaret E. Kuhn says, "Leadership also involves these functions: (1) putting down 'ground rules' about showing respect for all points of view and holding all members to the rule; (2) asking questions that point up differences and get all angles 'out into the open'; (3) helping the group as a whole to appreciate issues involved by frequent summaries or restatement of various points of view; (4) reminding group members that all human judgment stands under the judgment of God; (5) helping all to see that fellowship deepens and grows out of the experience of facing up to differences.

". . . in every controversial situation, understanding of the personalities involved is essential. Some people may deeply dislike each other, and carry their personal rancor into the discussion of the issue. Personal counseling may be needed outside the group."[3]

2. *Indecision.* Many groups have difficulty making decisions. They postpone action; they argue over insignificant details; they appoint subcommittees that go through the same decision-neurosis that the large group experienced. Some rush headlong into irresponsible vote-taking, only to reverse it at the next meeting. Some look for a miracle man to save them from making a decision.

Sometimes indecision occurs because of the fear of consequences. Will the church approve the action? What if the decision should be wrong? Do we know enough to make a decision?

In other cases, indecision is caused by conflicting loyalties. The differing loyalties of each individual group member were mentioned previously. The member may ask, "What will the other group think of me when they hear this decision?" A big step toward the solution is to get the group atmosphere to the place where its conflicts can be discussed without the element of threat.

The group will have taken another step toward maturity when it distinguishes between conflict in ideas and conflict based on likes and dislikes or feelings of insecurity. The second type of conflict must be recognized for what it is and dealt with or it will destroy the group.

The solution here is not an easy one. A clear thinking member of the group who feels no personal dislike or prejudice toward the conflicting members may be able to bring an understanding of the problem into clear focus. If he succeeds, he has performed a crucial leadership role. The appointed leader will try to promote an atmosphere where conflict on the issue is related to the decision-making process.

3. *Apathy*. Immaturity may crop up as marked indifference to the group task, or be vaguely discernible in lack of enthusiasm for the task—a symptom seen often enough in church groups to be disturbing.

Apathy may be detected in a variety of symptoms: lack of persistence in doing a job or satisfaction with shoddy work, frequent yawns, poor member participation, losing track of the point in discussion, lag in discussion, members come late or not at all, the group makes overquick decisions, there is reluctance to accept responsibility, failure to carry out decisions, eager suggestions for adjournment.

Frequently the designated leader is expected to provide inspiration and pep talks to build group morale and interest, but like the boy in the fable who called, "Wolf, wolf," these wear off quickly, and used too often completely lose their effectiveness. We must look deeper for the causes of apathy.

(1) One rather obvious cause for apathy may be the fact that the problem on which the group is working does not seem important to the members. It may be important to the leader, or the subgroup setting up the agenda, or "someone upstairs." The group members simply feel a meaningless task has been imposed on them. The problem here is that the group goal either is not clear, or is not shared by members.

(2) Or the problem may be important, but there are forces holding back the group from action. A local Christian education committee, for example, might avoid taking a significant action in their meeting because the pastor was absent and it was not clear what his attitude on the question might be. People avoid taking an action when they think it might open them to punishment. Groups get nowhere on some problems because of hostility toward certain members of the group. Sometimes the group climate does not invite honest participation. Silence then seems the safest course. In this case the group goal is not realistic because members are afraid to work toward it.

(3) Apathy may be the result of using poor group procedures for problem-solving. There may be a lack of understanding the steps needed in the process of decision-making, poor communication, failure to use facts—so that decisions turn out to be will-o'-the-wisps.

(4) A prolonged and deep fight between group members is a sure-fire way to produce apathy. Everything a group may wish to do can be overshadowed by a conflict between dominant members, or between members and the leader. When decisions are made by only a few members, the rest will tend to become apathetic.

4. *The Hidden Agenda.* An important danger in a group is that members may come to a meeting apparently to discuss a publicly stated agenda, but actually to work on a matter they do not bring out into the open.

An illustration might be a church workers' meeting to discuss plans for a teacher training session. The agenda item is a teacher training session for Thursday evening to run for ten weeks. Jack Glib doesn't say so, but he really wants to go bowling on Thursday night. Fanny Knowitall, a teacher in the public school system, feels this is a reflection on their ability as teachers. While she doesn't directly say so, she fights the idea of a teacher training session from this point of view. John Takeiteasy really doesn't want to get out of his easy chair on winter nights (he is careful not to say this). Each one of these persons has his own private agenda.

Hidden agendas can be held by individual members of the group, such as the group members mentioned above, by the leader, or by the group itself.

Hidden agendas may be focused on the leader and be expressed by competing with the leader to influence the group. A member, because of past unfortunate experiences, may feel generally hostile to all leaders. Consequently, he may use every opportunity to compete with the leader. Again it may be the very opposite, an excessive dependence on leadership.

Members may come to a meeting with "hip pocket" solutions to problems. They wait for the so-called "psychological moment" to have just thought of a good idea. Another member in an institutional organization may object to a plan for change because it threatens his job.

More often than may be suspected, designated leaders have hidden agendas. The leader, too, may have a hip pocket solution ready to insert when he feels the group has reached an impasse, or his purpose may be to maintain his leadership at any cost.

What is the leader's function in handling hidden agendas? The leader recognizes that his task is to help the group work on both its surface and its hidden agendas. He should recognize that hidden agendas may need to be worked on before progress can be made on the actual agenda. He recognizes that groups work on both levels simultaneously. He may at times help the group to bring the hidden agenda to the surface by saying something to this effect, "I wonder if we have said all we feel about this issue; perhaps we should go around the group to see if further thoughts can be opened up."

Ordinarily one should try to get hidden agendas before the group, but the wise leader must recognize that many hidden agendas cannot be talked about openly, because they would hurt the group more than they would help it. (There are, after all, some reasons for putting them under the table.) The leader must be sensitive enough to know what a group can and cannot handle at a given time.

The leader should not scold or pressure the group because of hidden agendas. They are not necessarily bad. They may be just as legitimate as the task at hand. Occasionally they may be more important than what the group has as its assignment.

The leader should help members of the group not to feel guilty about hidden agendas. He might say, for example, "It might be expected that we see things differently and should not feel guilty about wanting different things accomplished."

1. Lawrence K. Frank, *How to Be a Modern Leader* (New York: Association Press), p. 50. Quoted by permission.

2. From "Two Lessons in Group Dynamics," *Educator's Dispatch* (New York: Arthur C. Croft Publications), p. 4.

3. Margaret E. Kuhn, *You Can't Be Human Alone* (New York: Office of Publication and Distribution, 1956), p. 13.

Chapter 4

Getting Through to People

Teachers, superintendents, pastors, writers, and editors are in the communication business. If it is important for schoolteachers or business administrators to get their message across, it is more important for Christian workers to get the message of the Gospel through to people.

It seems strange that Christian workers have paid so little attention to the study of communication. Unfortunately, in some sections of the church, there seems to be an irresponsible attitude toward communication. One hears it reported, "It's our responsibility to preach the Gospel. It is God's business to convert people." It is, of course, true that only God can change the human heart, but it is a sobering responsibility to be the communicators of a message that can accomplish so much. Some Christians have a "take it or leave it attitude" about witnessing to the power of the Gospel. They seem to have no sense of shame, no sense of failure when people "leave it." As a matter of fact, many people do not accept the message of the Gospel because it is so poorly communicated to them. Did we really say it so that it was understood? Did we get ourselves sufficiently out of the way? Or did our acts or attitudes nullify all we said? It ought to be a matter of deep concern to all Christians when the Gospel is not received or believed.

For these reasons a study of communication is not merely a

matter of curious interest for teachers and church workers. It is near the center of many, if not all, of the church's activities. The importance of communication is being recognized in many areas. Psychiatrists are defining the function of psychotherapy in terms of restoring the communication process. That is to say what really happens to an emotionally disturbed person is that communication with the outside world has broken down. Anthropologists study communication patterns to understand the nature of a given society. Executives in big business put communication high on their agendas. They recognize that a proper image of the company must get through to people. The church, too, has big stakes in communicating a message effectively. It is heatening to see a growing concern about this problem in the church.

What Is Communication?

Stated simply, communication is the process of sharing with one or more persons an idea, feeling, or experience. We package our communications in books, pamphlets, conversation, discussion, pictures, radio, or television. When we *send* a communication, we may speak, draw, or write. When we *receive* a communication, we read, look, or listen. One expert on communication observed astutely, "Not what you say but what people think you say is communicated." This is a recognition of the fact that quite often people do not get what we intended to say.

It may be helpful to think of communication as a communication cable having various strands in it. Besides ideas, there are *feeling strands* in communication. Feelings are just as important as the words. Sometimes more important.

This indicates the need for making a distinction between verbal communication and nonverbal communication. Verbal communication uses sounds—spoken words or music. The strands in nonverbal communication are feelings, visual aids, pictures, and symbols. Feelings are an essential element of communication. Someone has said, "Feelings are facts." There are many feelings within us of which we are only partially aware. There is the need for acceptance. There are feelings of anxiety, of hostility, of dependence.

There is my feeling about the other person. My feeling about what he said and my feeling about myself. *How* a thing is said may on occasion be more important than *what* is said.

It is reported in the literature on communication that more than 60 per cent of communication is nonverbal. That is to say the largest part of communication does not involve the use of words at all. Leaders, therefore, must become increasingly sensitive to the many strands in communication. Leslie E. This writes, "Indeed, at times the most persuasive and important part of our communication apparatus is nonverbal: accent—manner of speech —gesture—facial expression—posture. A glance at one's watch during an interview, an impatient tapping with fingers—these cues may tell more about our feelings than words we use."[1]

Occasionally we are successful in getting a message through to the hearer. When we fail, some kind of barrier exists between the sender of the message and the receiver. Social scientists frequently use the following or a similar model of communication.

MODEL OF COMMUNICATION

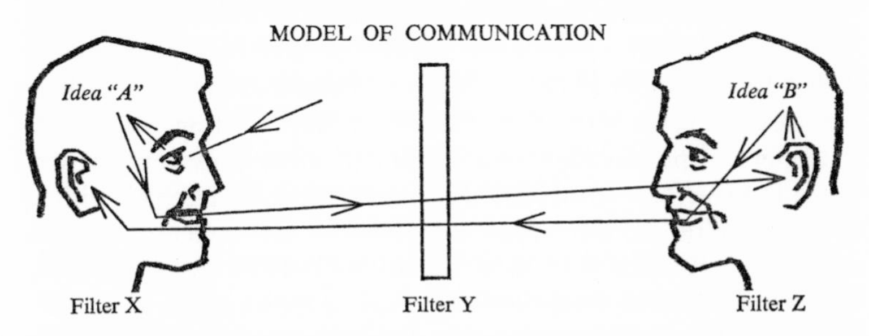

"A" represents an idea the person on the left wants to communicate to the person on the right. Filter "X" in the speaker causes him to tell only what he chooses to tell about it. "Z," an internal filter in the receiver of the message, filters out still more before the idea is received by the person on the right. Thus idea "A" is changed into idea "B," which represents what finally came through to the receiver. Filter "Y" represents external factors between the speaker and the listener that alter the communication. This model of communication will give us some idea of the complexity of communication.

Barriers to Communication

Let's discuss some common barriers to communication and relate them to the model of communication.

1. Internal barriers in the speaker (filter "X").

(1) Conscious assumptions about one's self in relation to other persons affect the quality of communication. For example, a person in a group may ask himself before speaking: Are my ideas wanted here? Are they worth expressing? Are others really interested in what I might have to say? Is there any use trying to communicate? Many persons struggle with questions like these. How they answer them affects their efforts to communicate. If the person feels others are not interested in his ideas, or that his contribution is not valuable, he probably will say little or nothing.

(2) Unconscious feelings about self in relation to others. If I talk, will I be punished? Is it "safe" to talk here? Is it "safe" to say I do not like my job, or that I do not like the conditions under which I work? Can I really trust my ideas or my feelings?

(3) The "clear only if known barrier." This barrier represents failure on the part of the speaker to give clear information. What he says is clear only if known. People encounter this barrier nearly everywhere. For example, in directions on how to use a camera. The directions are written to make sense only if you already know how to operate a camera. Most people have visited a strange city and have been compelled to ask directions to find their way. Perhaps they were told as one traveler was, "Take the main street into town and when you get to the city hall, turn left." The guide's directions were clear to himself, but the traveler did not know where the main street was or what the city hall looked like.

It is easy to overestimate people's knowledge. We assume that because we understand something clearly that others will understand it too. The Survey Research Center of the University of Michigan discovered that approximately 50 per cent of the American people do not recognize a cancer symptom, 50 per cent knew one symptom, 16 per cent recognized two symptoms, 7 per cent knew three symptoms, and only 3 per cent four or more symptoms. This suggests that in spite of all that has been done, public health officials still have a long hard pull to get cancer facts understood by people.

We are interested in getting people to understand and respond to the Gospel. They cannot respond to what they do not understand.

(4) The "words versus deeds barrier." This is the kind of barrier that can ruin effective communication for Christian workers. It has played havoc in the church's witness. We might conceivably buy a Ford from a salesman who came to our home driving a Chevrolet, but people generally have trouble when "what you do speaks so loud they cannot hear what you say" in matters of the Christian faith.

One of the most effective ways parents, leaders, church workers can communicate the Christian faith is to practice it! Somehow it is easier to comprehend the truths of the Christian faith when they are clothed with deeds. That's what God did when He sent His Son into the world. In writing to Titus Paul said, "That they may adorn the doctrine of God our Saviour in all things" (Titus 2:10). That means put clothes on what you believe.

Writers on public school education are quick to observe that superintendents of public instruction cannot communicate the importance of democracy to teachers when their staff meetings are authoritarian. A teacher in a public school classroom cannot teach democracy when her methods are undemocratic. Neither can a Christian teacher effectively teach the Christian faith so long as it is merely an intellectual concept. The creed must become deed. The surest way to find out what love is, is to see it practiced.

2. There are barriers between the speaker and the listener (filter "Y").

(1) There are physical barriers to communication. Examples of such barriers are faulty radio reception or inability to hear. Maybe Mr. Kaufman didn't get a copy of the evening paper and consequently missed a notice of an evening meeting because the paper boy forgot him or the children grabbed the paper first.

Physical barriers operate in the work of the church too. How will the teachers know about a teachers' meeting or workers' conference if the superintendent didn't tell them about it on time?

How can the teachers know about opportunities for self-improvement or a class project if the superintendent keeps such information on his desk?

Occasionally Sunday-school teachers are encouraged to send home letters and take-home activities with children. The letters are intended to interpret the program of the Sunday school. However, children do not always take things home. Lack of co-operation may occur because parents actually didn't get the letters. To avoid such situations parents should perhaps in some cases be contacted directly.

If, for example, the teacher is teaching a Sunday-school class competing with a babble of voices around him, communication will be difficult. When people can't hear what is being said, attention wanders. When a neighboring voice booms through stronger than that of the teacher, attention will drift to that voice. Discussion particularly will be well-nigh impossible under such circumstances because members of the class cannot hear what is being said by other members.

(2) The language barrier. Social scientists who have studied the matter say that no two people get identical meanings from the same words. This happens because people do not have identical experiences. Because we have common experiences about oranges, bananas, tables, or chairs, we can communicate quite adequately about these things. But abstractions like communism, democracy, curriculum, or philosophy leave us open to differing understandings and interpretations.

Because language is so closely related to feelings, it is often used to conceal meaning rather than to reveal it. What do people usually say when the boss asks them how they like their job? (You might get fired if you didn't like your job.) Think of a family pausing at the door of a friend's home before departing to express their courtesies after enduring an evening's showing of their friend's vacation slides.

Semantic problems increase when we talk to the public. There is even less common ground for understanding. For example, the public may see little difference between *discussing* socialism and *advocating* it. They may see no difference in *reporting* the Vatican

Council and *endorsing* it. Editors of church papers can furnish illustrations of such misreadings.

One way to overcome the semantic barrier is to explain abstractions. For example, if the Sunday-school superintendent says that children need more discipline, he had better say what he means by discipline or some teachers and parents will think he advocates getting a bundle of hickory sticks.

(3) The jargon barrier. The jargon barrier is related to the language barrier. Rudolf Flesch in *The Art of Plain Talk* quotes the following income tax instructions which every citizen is supposed to know how to read whether he wants to or not.

> (3) Substantial Underestimate of Estimated Tax.—In the case of individuals other than farmers, if 80 per cent of the tax (determined without regard to the credits for tax withheld on tax-free covenant bonds and for Income and Victory Tax withheld on wages) exceeds the estimated tax (increased by such credits), and in the case of farmers, if 66 2/3 per cent of the tax (determined without regard to such credits) exceeds the estimated tax (increased by such credits), there shall be added to the tax an amount equal to such excess, or equal to 6 per cent of the amount by which the tax so determined exceeds the estimated tax so increased, whichever is the lesser.[2]

The following are Flesch's comments on this monster: "Next time you get around to tax paying you will have to read and understand sentences like this; right now, you may just look at it for a while the way you would look at a dinosaur skeleton in a museum. As your guide, I can tell you that it contains 107 words, 21 prepositions, 11 past participles, and 8 places where you have to do some arithmetic. And just to save you a sleepless night, here is the gist of it: If you guess your tax too low, you'll have to pay a fine but they can't fine you more than 6 per cent of your error."[3]

Technical terminology is a short cut for communicating within specialized groups. The use of jargon not only blocks the message; what is worse it sets up emotional fences as well. People react by saying things like this: Why does the stuffed shirt have to pontificate that "a state of incipient baldness exists when the rate of hair fall exceeds the rate of hair replacement," when he might have said, "When your hair falls out faster than it grows in, brother, you are getting bald."

"In communicating with the public, let us take Aristotle's advice and think like wise men but talk simply. It isn't easy. After the air is cleared of polysyllabic obfuscation, we are often left with rather simple ideas and sometimes we are left with no ideas at all. Big words conceal little thoughts."[4]

(4) Barriers of time and space. Christian workers particularly have problems in communicating the message of the Gospel because of the barriers of time and space. Christianity was cradled in Judaism many centuries ago in a land far away. We try to communicate to children the acts of God in history. Our problem and our challenge is to make sacred history intelligible to this generation.

(5) The barriers of class and culture. Christian workers are faced with the problem of translating meanings across lines of class and culture. First we face the difficulty of understanding today the message of the Bible which was nurtured in a different culture. When we take the Gospel message to other countries, we again face the problem of translating the message into the different culture. Sometimes missionaries discover that people in Eastern countries understand some things about ancient Biblical culture better than Westerners do.

Eugene Nida tells of the problem of translating portions of the New Testament for certain African tribes. He referred to a problem they had in translating the story of the publican and the Pharisee. Where our translation says that the publican smote his breast, the meaning is lost on certain African tribes because to smite one's breast is like putting one's finger under a coat lapel; it's an expression of pride and smug self-complacency—the opposite of what the actions of the publican are supposed to convey. To make the action suit the thought, in the African translation the African should beat his head with his hands.

3. Barriers internal to the listener (filter "Z").

(1) Stereotype barriers. The word "stereotype" is used by social psychologists to mean the picture in people's heads. They

insist we do not see and hear "what is out there," but we see and hear a combination of "what is out there" and "what is in our heads." Another way of saying it is that we are predisposed to hear what we want to hear. We tend to hear what we want to hear about the Bible. We hear what we want to hear about the merit of translations of the Bible. We tend to hear what we want to hear about political parties. We hear what we want to hear about the National Council of Churches or National Association of Evangelicals. If we have feelings of ill will towards certain persons, we tend to hear only the bad things about them.

The pictures in our heads are formed by our interests, attitudes, and prejudices. This filter works in our seeing, our hearing, and reporting. Our attention is selective. We pay attention to those things in which we are interested. A small boy on entering a dentist's office sees "the comic book." His mother sees *The Ladies' Home Journal.*

The fact that people tend to see and hear what they are interested in seems to the Christian worker to illustrate the Scripture, "To him that hath shall be given and from him that hath not shall be taken even that which he has." A lack of interest can block communication. This accents the fact that one of the teacher's biggest jobs is to motivate pupils—to get them to want to do what they ought to do.

What We Can Do to Remove Communication Barriers

1. One of the simplest things and in some ways the easiest thing we can do to improve communication is to remove the physical barriers. Make sure the room in which the group gathers is comfortable. Make it possible for persons to see and to hear. (There are definite rules about setting up a projection screen for viewing, for example.) Get announcements out on time.

2. Clarify and simplify ideas before presenting them. Illustrations help to clarify our meanings. Nothing is so complex but what it can't be made simpler.

3. Work for two-way communication. The complete cycle of communication involves a three-step process. Here is person *A*

who hurls a communication over to person *B*. Obviously we need to ask, Did *B* get it? Somebody has to reveal something and someone else has to listen to it. There is no real communication unless the sender and the receiver are interacting, but the process of communication is not complete until *B* reports back to *A* that he has heard and understood.

It is a thrilling experience for a teacher or a minister to hear someone play back accurately and clearly an idea he tried to communicate. There is something personally rewarding in the knowledge that we are understood. But unless we test the effectiveness of our communication by securing two-way communication, we will not know whether our ideas are understood.

Lectures are notoriously poor methods for communication. The listener has no opportunity to test whether he understood the speaker correctly. On the other hand, question periods and discussion sessions will help to clarify ideas. It is one way of being sure we understood what the speaker said. Discussion also helps insure that ideas being exchanged are getting down to the interest level of the group.

4. Often barriers to communication can be removed by developing a permissive, nonjudgmental atmosphere through acceptance of self and others as the children of God with ideas that need to be listened to and feelings that need to be expressed.

1. Leslie E. This, *The Leader Looks at Communication* (Washington: Leadership Resources, Inc., 1961), p. 5.
2. Rudolf Flesch, *The Art of Plain Talk* (New York: Harper & Brothers, 1946), p. 9.
3. *Ibid.*
4. *Portfolio of Teaching Techniques,* No. 1 (Connecticut: Arthur C. Croft Publications, 1955), p. 38.

Chapter 5

Who Does What and Why?

All groups whether they are committees, a Sunday-school class, a parent-teacher meeting, or a church board have certain common characteristics. To understand how individual members of a group can function effectively in a group, it will be helpful to examine some of the characteristics of group life. These characteristics are found in the groups to which we belong. Most groups come together for a purpose. They are working toward some goal.

Ways of Looking at Groups

1. Group background. Persons who come to a new group do not come completely neutral. Each member comes to the meeting with a particular mind-set. Every group and each person in the group has a history. Each member comes to the group with preconceived notions—a certain bias and attitude which will have a bearing on what he will do and will influence the way the group will function. For example, a person attending a workers' conference may be wondering, "When will this meeting be over?" Or he may come to the meeting thinking, "I am not going to let that teacher pull something over on me this time."

2. Group participation patterns. Persons participate in a group by speaking to each other. When one person speaks 50 per cent of the time, it cuts down drastically the amount of time for other participants. To which individuals are remarks addressed?

What does this tell us about status and power in the group? A point not to be neglected is how much talking is done by the designated leader. General participation is desirable so long as it is appropriate to the task and within the resources of the members.

3. Group communication patterns. Persons communicate with each other in a variety of ways. This refers to what people say, how they say it, and what effect it has on other members of the group. This suggests the importance of recognizing nonverbal communication—facial expressions, posture, and general attitudes. Often people "speak past each other." This is an indication that they are not really listening. If a member is reading a newspaper at a meeting, he will hardly need to tell anyone that he is bored. This is nonverbal communication.

4. Group cohesion. This relates to the attractiveness of a group to its members. The way a group "sticks together" has a bearing on its efficiency, its ability to make decisions,—and most important—on the commitment of its members in following through on a decision. Common fear of an enemy or zeal for a given task strengthens the cohesiveness of a group. The kind of cohesiveness to work for is to have members of the group working together in an interdependent way, each being free to contribute his best to the task.

5. Subgroups. We ordinarily refer to subgroups as cliques. Cliques form on the basis of friendship, common interest, or common feeling against a member or a common concern about the direction in which the group is moving.

It would be reassuring to think that cliques do not exist in church groups, but, alas, they are as common as Kansas sunflowers. One of the problems for the group, and especially the designated leader, is to deal with cliques in such a way as not to cut them off or isolate them, but bring them back into the group.

6. Group atmosphere. This refers to the degree of freedom and informality in the group. Is the atmosphere permissive and friendly, or is it a controlling, punishing, rigid one? Can members express themselves honestly? Do people say what they think or do they say what is expected? The kind of atmosphere to work for is one in which members feel free to speak.

7. Group goals. Every group is working toward some kind of goal. Clarify or lack of clarity about group goals will directly affect the work of a group. Members may disagree on what the goal is. In other cases the goal may be ambiguous. Each of these situations is a danger signal for group life.

8. Group standards. Each group adopts its own ways of operating; it sets up its own boundaries and limitations on the way in which it carries out its work. One of the first tasks of a Sunday-school teacher is to work for the acceptance of group standards: Will the pupils come on time? May they throw erasers and spit-balls? May they whisper or not pay attention to the teacher? How do they address the teacher?

9. The designated leader. Most groups have someone who is the designated leader. He shares his leadership functions with members of the group. The purpose of this entire unit is to get a clearer understanding of what leadership functions are.

10. Member behavior. The effectiveness of group functioning will depend on how the members contribute to the task of reaching the accepted goals. In the remaining part of this session, we will examine more carefully how the designated leader shares responsibility of leadership with members and what the members' leadership roles are.

On Three Levels

Against this background we may look at a group from a different perspective. We previously observed that every group functions on three levels:

1. The task level. Most groups exist for the purpose of getting a job done. It may range from quilting, choir practice, teaching a class, to a session on a conference floor. Many church groups operate mainly on the task level. They are task-oriented. They are so occupied with the job to be done that they tend not to be aware of other "needs" within the group.

2. Maintenance level. Because there is constant interaction in a group, the exchanges may sometimes be rather disruptive. The group then faces the need for mending broken relationships if it is to get its task done. The maintenance level pertains to what

is happening to people while the task is being done. Often we ride rough shod over people in order to get the job done. This is especially unfortunate within the Christian fellowship. In the Christian brotherhood one of our major concerns should be persons and what happens to them.

3. Individual needs level. Each member comes to the group with his peculiar individual needs. They may range from picking the easiest chair within reach or doodling, to blocking action, or attempting to dominate the group. The member's behavior may be motivated by the desire to secure recognition. In that case he will work at it in various ways. He may make extreme or shocking statements. He may talk excessively. Or he may challenge the designated leader. The individual needs level is the one that most often goes unrecognized because members of the group tend to be task-centered.

The mature group learns to operate on all three levels and keep them in proper balance. It recognizes that if one of these levels—for example, individual needs—is neglected the efficiency of the group is impaired. There are certain tensions that operate here. The more emphasis the group puts on getting its task accomplished, the less it is inclined to pay attention to individual needs. On the other hand when the group gives too much attention to individual needs, the task suffers. The leader is constantly faced with the problem of giving proper emphasis to each of these three levels. He must see that the task needs are met without hurting persons and see to it that meeting individual needs does not result in failure to get the task accomplished.

Members of a group, like a basketball team, should learn how to function together effectively. They need to learn what equipment, knowledge, and skills the job calls for. The members should be able to perform the roles the job requires.

For a group to function properly at all three levels described above, a number of leadership functions must be performed by both the designated leader and the members of the group. Depending upon the situation, these group member functions will help the group satisfy the needs of its members and help it move toward its objectives.

Different Functions at Different Times

Following is a description of member roles:[1]

1. *Roles that are task-centered.* These are the functions needed to select and carry out a task.

(1) *Initiating activity.* This may be a proposal for a solution or suggesting a new idea for consideration. The initiator may add a new dimension to a definition. For example, when a group is stalemated, the member may say, 'I suggest we use the following procedure to get at this problem."

(2) *Information seeking.* Groups frequently have insufficient information to deal adequately with a question. The information seeker performs the role of getting the information to the group. He may also get before the group a request for clarification.

(3) *Opinion giving.* The opinion giver may share his opinion or state his belief about the question being discussed. His concern is about values rather than about facts.

(4) *Information giving.* A member who takes this role offers facts or generalizations, sometimes relating to his personal experience to add additional light.

(5) *Clarifying.* In every group there are misunderstandings and unclear meaning. The clarifier tries to interpret meanings, to envision how a proposal might work out if adopted. He attempts to clear up confusion and points out alternatives. He may on occasion provide an example.

(6) *Summarizing.* The summarizer tries to pull together what was said so that the group can see more clearly the progress or lack of progress made. He may crystallize his summary statement to offer a decision or conclusion for group consideration.

(7) *Consensus testing.* Sometimes it is really difficult to know what a group is saying. The tester for consensus sends up a trial balloon. He may say, "As I heard the discussion, this is what we are saying. . . ." He is attempting to discover how much agreement has been reached.

2. *Roles that are group-centered (maintenance roles).* These are the functions required to strengthen and maintain group life.

(1) *Encouraging.* This role can be taken by members with complete sincerity by being friendly, warm, and responsive to

others, agreeing with and accepting the contributions of others where possible.

(2) *Gatekeeping.* This function is expressed in a concern about the way members participate in the group. Some members of the group may be silent. Sometimes the "gatekeeper" invites another member of the group to make a contribution. The member may say, "We haven't heard a thing from Mabel yet. . . . What do you think about? . . ." Or he may suggest a limited talking time for everyone in order to head off a monopolizer of conversation in order to give others a chance to contribute.

(3) *Harmonizing.* There will always be opportunity to harmonize disagreements within groups. The harmonizer tries to get people to explore their differences a little more carefully. It may be they are just looking at a problem from different perspectives.

(4) *Compromising.* Compromising is not always bad. Occasionally when one's own ideas are involved in a conflict it becomes necessary to compromise one's own position. It may indicate admitting error. Always it is disciplining one's self to do the necessary function to maintain the group.

(5) *Tension relieving.* As different opinions are expressed, and conflicting positions are taken by members, it is inevitable that tension builds up. Many groups are fortunate in having one or more members who can take tension-relieving roles. He may introduce a bit of humor just at the right time or he may lift up the ridiculous side of a serious conflict.

3. *Roles that are self-centered (individual need level).*

(1) The aggressor works in devious ways not always clearly recognizable on the surface. The following characteristics identify him: he acts in ways calculated to deflate the status of others; he may express disapproval of values held by the group. For example, he might discount the importance of regular church attendance. He may attack the problem the group is working on or attack the group itself. He may joke aggressively or show envy for another member's contribution by taking credit for it himself.

(2) The playboy displays his lack of involvement in the group by making cynical remarks, taking on an "I don't care" attitude, and by horseplay.

(3) The special interest pleader speaks for the small businessman, the housewife, the common man—usually cloaking his own prejudices or biases in the stereotype which best suits his needs at the moment.

(4) The blocker tends to be stubbornly resistant, disagreeing or opposing beyond reason. He may try to bring back an issue the group has already disposed of. Occasionally he is harder to recognize. He may block when he didn't intend to. He may talk an idea to death by being too anxious to push an idea through and thereby kill its chances of acceptance.

(5) The self-confessor uses the group as an audience to express his personal "feelings" or "insights."

(6) The dominator attempts to maintain a superior position in the group. His attempts at domination may take the form of flattery, asserting status, right to attention, interrupting others, giving directions officiously.

(7) The help seeker tries to gain sympathy from other group members by expressing insecurity, by personal confession, or by depreciating himself beyond reason.

Summary

A quotation from Leland P. Bradford and Gordon L. Lippitt serves admirably as a summary to this discussion: "A group requires at different times many different kinds of contributions. Ideas need to be presented, differing opinions need bridging, suggestions need reality testing, procedures need to be recommended, support to hesitant members needs to be given, group direction needs to be checked and tension reduced.

"These roles have been defined in three large categories: task-centered, group-centered, and individual-centered functions. At different times the group needs contributions from its members in each of these categories. Unless they are made at the appropriate time, the group suffers and its task is less effectively completed.

"The important concept gained from this research is that we need to understand the wide variety of needed member contributions for effective group operation and the opportunity presented for great differences among individuals in their contributions. . . .

"Ineffective groups are those in which the leader plays a variety of roles—moderator, summarizer, arbitrator, policeman, reporter, suggester of ideas—while members are supposed to confine their contributions to a limited pattern. Anyone breaking through this rigid mold is seen as a disrupter.

"An effective group permits individuals to behave in accordance with their own personality and needs, as well as in regard to the wide range of group needs. By the individual's becoming aware of his role and of the group's sensitivity to the needs of the situation, effective human relations can take place."[2]

Are such roles required in Christian groups? Have you observed these functions in groups to which you belong? Can we identify a person in a group who attempts to be understanding and helpful? Perhaps more often we have seen Christian groups flounder and relationships become bitter because group members did not exercise these roles. By putting into practice these member functions we may experience in a new and fresh way what a redemptive fellowship is. When an entire group seeks with understanding, intelligence, love, and forbearance to "take in" an immature member, they will experience the meaning of redemptive fellowship.

1. Following Benne and Sheats.

2. Leland P. Bradford and Gordon L. Lippitt, "The Individual Counts in Effective Group Relations," from *NEA Journal,* November, 1954. Quoted by permission.

Chapter 6

Marks of a Mature Group

We take up this study after we have had an opportunity to gain some background for understanding how groups work and get things done. We gained some insights into what makes groups immature and what are some of the characteristics of groups in which we serve.

Appraising the maturity level of a group is not an easy task. There is some agreement and much disagreement among people who do research on groups on this subject. Much depends on the point of view taken. For example, one might say that if a group solves problems in a highly satisfactory way, it is a "good group." Or we might say that if the members like the group, it is a mature group. However, there are some elusive factors here.

It may not necessarily be a good group because we get satisfactions from it. Not all of what appears as fellowship is true Christian fellowship. Some of the satisfactions could conceivably come from trying to dominate the group. Sometimes groups succeed in getting the task done all right, but they steam roller people in getting the job done. This should help us to see that quite a number of elements need to be considered in appraising the effectiveness of a group.

Characteristics of Mature Groups

1. One of the marks of a mature group is the clarity of the

group goal. Most groups exist for the sole purpose of getting specific tasks done. A temporary committee may have as its purpose the selection and purchase of a suitable gift to be presented on the occasion of Miss Miller's twenty-fifth year of teaching in the Sunday school. Or it might be a committee selected to work out plans for building a new church.

How such committees get their jobs done depends on a number of factors. It will depend in part upon having a goal that is obtainable. A goal should be clearly understood by all. A goal should be accepted by the group and modified by the group, if necessary. The goals are not decided by the leader who then attempts to impose them upon the group.

Because human nature is essentially the same everywhere, conditions affecting the effective functioning of the group life apply to any group anywhere at any time. Ideas, educational levels, cultural background, and habit patterns may vary, but feelings are surprisingly universal. Persons have feelings of fear, faith, hate, love, jealousy, guilt, loneliness, and frustration. All persons seek freedom, acceptance, a sense of belonging, recognition, a sense of achievement, new experiences, and security. All want to realize their potential dignity as persons and not be treated as things.

2. Successful group productivity depends on the ability of members to exchange ideas freely in a permissive atmosphere. The members must feel involved in the decisions and the process of the group.

A permissive atmosphere is one where members are free to express their opinions. The expression of individual differences of opinion, as we pointed out previously, are made more easily in a permissive atmosphere than in an autocratic, manipulated one. The atmosphere of the group is important in determining whether an individual feels free to speak honestly and frankly. It not only encourages members to participate when they are ready, but it makes it seem more natural and easier for them to express their ideas. Haven't we all found that it is admittedly difficult to speak when someone is glowering at us?

A collection of able people does not assure a smooth functioning group. A committee of mature adults may make a very immature working group. When a new group forms, it may develop into a mature working group, or it may fail to grow up in the way it gets things done.

The failure of a group to function properly is not necessarily the fault of a leader. No group can move toward maturity until all members are willing to assume mature responsibility for the way members act.

It frequently happens in meetings of church groups that feelings and differences of opinion remain unspoken throughout the meeting. Later, it comes out that a number of persons in the group have strong negative feelings about the meeting. This then disrupts and even delays the problem-solving process of the group.

Nearly everyone reading this can recall meetings in which member participation was poor. But after the meeting, people talked up and it turned out that a number of people expressed strong feelings against the action taken by the group. Why didn't they speak in the meeting?

We find it difficult to accord others complete freedom to express their ideas. James counseled Christians of the early days, "Speak not evil of one another, brethren. He that speaketh evil of his brother, and judgeth his brother, speaketh evil of the law, and judgeth the law: but if thou judge the law, thou art not a doer of the law but a judge. There is one lawgiver, who is able to save and to destroy; who art thou that judgeth another" (Jas. 4:11, 12)?

Commenting upon the freedom we should allow our brothers in Christ, Dietrich Bonhoeffer says, "Where this discipline of the tongue is practiced right from the beginning, each individual will make a matchless discovery. He will be able to cease from constantly scrutinizing the other person, judging him, condemning him, putting him in his particular place where he can gain ascendancy over him and thus doing violence to him as a person. Now he can allow the brother to exist as a completely free person, as God made him to be. His view expands and, to his amazement, for the first time he sees, shining above his brethren, the richness of God's creative glory. God did not make this person as I would have made him. He did not give him to me as a brother for me to dominate and control, but in order that I may find above him the Creator. Now the other person, in the freedom with which he was created, becomes the occasion of joy, whereas before he was only a nuisance and affliction. God does not will that I should fashion the other person according to the image that seems good to me, that is, in my own image; rather in his very freedom from me God made this person in His image. I can never know beforehand how God's image should appear in others . . . to me the sight may seem strange, even ungodly. But God creates every man in the likeness of His Son who was crucified. After all, even that image certainly looked strange and ungodly to me before I grasped it.

"Strong and weak, wise and foolish, gifted or ungifted, pious or impious, diverse individuals in the community, are no longer incentives for talking and judging and condemning, and thus excuses for self-justification. They are rather cause for rejoicing in one another and serving one another. . . .

"In a Christian community everything depends on whether each individual is an indispensable link in a chain. Only when the smallest link is securely interlocked is the chain unbreakable. A community which allows unemployed members to exist within it will perish because of them. . . . Every Christian community must realize that not only do the weak need the strong, but also that the strong cannot exist without the weak. The elimination of the weak is the death of the fellowship."[1]

3. Members of mature groups have learned to listen carefully. Most of us are poor listeners. The art of listening can be improved. We are probably all in need of the injunction to talk less and to listen more. God gave you only *one* mouth, but he gave you *two* ears. Watch for feelings accompanying the words. Listen to the tones in which words are spoken. Ask yourself: What is this person *really* saying? Is he asking for attention, understanding, sympathy, acceptance? Is he expressing opposition? Does he want reassurance, punishment, or advice?

Writing about the Christian ministry of listening, Dietrich Bonhoeffer again wisely notes, "Many people are looking for an ear that will listen. They do not find it among Christians, because these Christians are talking where they should be listening. But he who can no longer listen to his brother will be no longer listening to God either; he will be doing nothing but prattle in the presence of God too. This is the beginning of the death of the spiritual life, and in the end there is nothing left but spiritual chatter and clerical condensation arrayed in pious words. One who cannot listen long and patiently will presently be talking beside the point and be never really speaking to others, albeit he is not conscious of it. Anyone who thinks that his time is too valuable to spend in keeping quiet will eventually have no time for God and his brother, but only for himself and for his own follies. . . .

"Secular education today is aware that often a person can be helped merely by having someone who will listen to him seriously, and upon this insight it has constructed its soul therapy, which has attracted great numbers of people, including Christians. But Christians have forgotten that the ministry of listening has been committed to them by Him who is Himself the greatest listener and whose work they should share. We should listen with the ears of God so that we may speak the Word of God."[2]

4. Members of mature groups have grown in their ability to absorb hostility. One wonders whether those of us who give lip service to the peace position have learned the art of absorbing hostility. Frequently in the groups with which we meet, discussions never rise above the "emotional level." We find it difficult to dis-associate the idea a person expresses from the person. Many rifts within the church occurred on the personality level rather than because of actual significant doctrinal differences.

Jesse Ziegler, who has given much time and effort to the group relations movement, writing on this point, says, "Learn to absorb hostility, especially when it is aimed at you. Don't argue, don't accuse, don't be defensive. Smile, keep quiet, listen patiently. When the other person finally runs out of words, say honsetly, 'I understand how you feel.' Then, restate his accusations accurately so that he realizes that you really do understand him. Then, where necessary, add calmly, 'Although I understand you, and just how you feel, I cannot agree with your conclusions because. . . .' "

Absorbing hostility in a group is like smothering with one's own body the burning firebrand thrown into a highly inflammable environment. Not to meet hostility with hatred is a signficant victory for a Christian. In a group it is doubly significant because hostilities tend to spread like prairie fires and they are almost as hard to control. Those, who by God's help, have absorbed hostility have known that it can bring exhilaration never thought possible.

We are admonished in the New Testament, "Bear ye one another's burdens, and so fulfil the law of Christ" (Gal. 6:2). Again Dietrich Bonhoeffer points out that "bearing" here means forbearing and sustaining. "The brother is a burden to the Christian precisely because he is the Christian. For the pagan the other person never becomes a burden at all. He simply sidesteps every burden that others may impose upon him.

"The Christian, however, must bear the burden of a brother. He must suffer and endure the brother. It is only when he is a burden that another person is really a brother and not merely an object to be manipulated. The burden of men was so heavy for God Himself that He had to endure the cross. God verily bore the burden of men in the body of Jesus Christ. But He bore them as a mother carries her child, as a shepherd enfolds the lost lamb that has been found. God took men upon Himself and they weighted Him to the ground, but God remained with them and they with God. In bearing with men God maintained fellowship with them. It is the law of Christ that was fulfilled in the cross and Christians must share in this law. They must suffer their brethren, but, what is more important, now that the law of Christ has been fulfilled they *can* bear with their brethren."[3]

"It is, first of all, the *freedom* of the other person, of which we spoke earlier, that is a burden to the Christian. The other's freedom collides with his own autonomy, yet he must recognize it. He could get rid of this burden by refusing the other person his freedom, by constraining him and thus doing violence to his personality, by stamping his own image upon him. But if he lets God create His image in him, he by this token gives him his freedom and himself bears the burden of this freedom of another creature of God. The freedom of the other person includes all that we mean by a person's nature, individuality, endowment. It also includes his weakness and oddities, which are such a trial to our patience, everything that produces frictions, conflicts, and collisions among us. To bear the burden of the other person means involvement with the created reality of the other, to accept and affirm it, and, in bearing with it, to break through to the point where we take joy in it."[4]

"Then, besides the other's freedom, there is the abuse of that freedom that becomes a burden for the Christian. The sin of the other person is harder to bear than his freedom; for in sin, fellowship with God and with the brother is broken. Here the Christian suffers the rupture of his fellowship with the other person that had its basis in Jesus Christ, but here, too, it is only in bearing with him that the great grace of God becomes wholly plain. To cherish no contempt for the sinner but rather to prize the privilege of bearing him means not to have to give him up as lost, to be able to accept him, to preserve fellowship with him through forgiveness. 'Brethren, if a man be overtaken in a fault, ye which are spiritual, restore such an one in the spirit of meekness' (Gal. 6:1). As Christ bore and received us sinners so we in His fellowship may bear and receive sinners into the fellowship of Jesus Christ through the forgiving of sins."[5]

5. Mature groups recognize the value of compromise. It stands to reason that when a number of people work on the solution of a problem, varying viewpoints will be presented. Members of the group will have specialized resources to bring to bear on the problems at hand. A proposal made by one member may need to be modified in the light of additional facts contributed by other members of the group.

Take, for example, a committee meeting to select a gift for Miss Elsie Brubaker, a retiring teacher. In the meeting there were a number of suggestions for a gift. Finally, Mary White suggested, "Why doesn't one of us talk to her informally and find out what she needs without letting on." This seemed a good suggestion and was about to be accepted when Janet Boswell said, "It would be too obvious for someone to talk to her about what she needed for a trip. To talk about needing a suitcase or a new coat or a hat would give it away. Why don't we ask one of her personal friends?

Then the gift will be a complete surprise." This suggestion was incorporated into the final solution. It illustrates the element of compromise so often necessary in properly functioning groups.

6. Mature groups are sensitive to the needs of members. The kinds of individual needs that may be represented in the group have been described previously. Groups within the church with a concern for persons should be expected to give consideration to individual needs but this frequently does not happen. Instead, members of a group are lined up against each other by vote taking. They are dominated by leaders, or they are completely task-dominated. Too often the slogan seems to be: "Let's get the job done. People can take care of themselves."

Writing about this problem in churches, Cynthia C. Wedel says, "A second requirement for a good group is for those involved to become aware of procedures used. Even the most task-centered secular group—a committee which has come together to plan a community event or to solve a business problem—often finds the accomplishment of its task hindered or stopped by lack of attention to process. Unclear goals, lack of participation, tensions between individuals, may make the achievement of the task impossible.

"It is even more important in church groups, where relationships are a primary concern and means are as important as ends, that we become aware of the process by which we are doing our work. There is something wrong about a group which carries out a successful project, but in the course of it allows two or three people to be hurt or rejected; or one in which all decisions are made by majority vote with no consideration given to the minority point of view."[6]

7. Mature groups develop the ability to make decisions by consensus. Vote taking tends to commit members to a position by disregarding the minority position. In the classroom, too, the teacher who hands down the answers will not get the kind of receptivity to new ideas that persons who engage in a common discussion and search for answers to problems will have. It may not always be possible to reach consensus, but it is more realistic than vote taking. This will be discussed more fully later.

8. An effective group allows for a sharing of leadership responsibility by group members so that all members are involved in contributing ideas, elaborating and clarifying the ideas of others, giving opinions, testing feasibility, and assisting the group to maintain itself.

Paul F. Douglass observes, "If wholeness in participation is a goal, how can one judge the contribution a person makes when it is clearly recognized that every human being differs from every other in his abilities? How is one to judge the quantity or quality of performance? Jesus recognized this problem too. By way of answer He cited the widow and her mite. Here was a human being who performed to the level of her ability. Jesus' answer was that what makes an act acceptable and divine is total performance with resource a person can bring to the task."[7]

Here follows a summary of the contrasts between a mature and an immature group as given by W. Randolph Thornton in an article entitled "Guarding Group Growth."

Immature Group Actions	*Mature Group Behavior*
1. The atmosphere is stiff and formal. People address each other as Miss Jones or Dr. Smith.	1. The atmosphere is informal and permissive. Members address each other as Mary or John.
2. Individuals are judged by wealth, clothes, degrees, or status in other groups.	2. Members are judged by the value of their contributions to this group.
3. Each person is so busy thinking of what he wants to say next that he doesn't listen to the others.	3. Members listen attentively and watch for behavioral cues as others speak.
4. Members fear expressions of hostility and are very polite to one another.	4. Members are frank because the group can absorb large amounts of hostility without becoming disrupted.
5. Members avoid controversial issues for fear of splitting the group.	5. The group deals with controversial issues without becoming antagonistic.

6. The group concentrates on the subject matter and ignores its own processes.

6. While dealing with subject matter, the members keep aware of process. An official observer is also appointed.

7. Opinions are expressed before the task is clarified or facts secured.

7. Before expressing opinions members ask questions to clarify the task and gain information.

8. As soon as a proposal is presented, it is torn apart or refuted.

8. Members try to find some aspect of every proposal with which they can agree; then they build on that aspect.

9. Compromise is regarded as undesirable.

9. Compromise is seen as a useful tool for securing agreement.

10. The group either ignores its silent members or tries to force them to talk.

10. The group tries to use the talents of all members by providing opportunity for full participation, but never insists that a member must speak.

11. Motions are made early in the discussion and decisions are reached by voting.

11. Members try to avoid motions and voting; instead, they seek to reach decisions by consensus.

12. Individuals tend to reject those who disagree with them, or those who disagree with the majority.

12. The group accepts every member regardless of his views, and tries to use his every contribution.

13. The group is unaware of the personal needs of its members and, therefore, unable to meet these needs.

13. The group, being aware that certain members have a strong need for recognition or security, tries to satisfy such needs in a way which contributes to the group purpose.

14. Individuals tend to perform only one role, such as fa-

14. Each member performs various roles as needed by the

voring every proposal or opposing everything.

15. The matter of guiding the group is left to the leader who receives credit for success and blame for failure.

group, such as clarifying, harmonizing, or summarizing.

15. Members also feel responsible for guiding the group and therefore share many leadership functions.[8]

1. Dietrich Bonhoeffer, *Life Together* (New York: Harper & Brothers Publishers, 1954), pp. 92-94.
2. *Ibid.*, pp. 97-99.
3. *Ibid.*, p. 100.
4. *Ibid.*, p. 101.
5. *Ibid.*, p. 102.
6. Cynthia C. Wedel, "Group Life in the Church," *The International Journal of Religious Education* (May 1957), p. 14.
7. Paul F. Douglass, *The Group Workshop Way in the Church* (New York: Association Press), p. 83.
8. W. Randolph Thornton, reprinted from *Bethany Guide* by permission.

Chapter 7

An Atmosphere of Love and Redemption

Group atmosphere is an expression used to describe the emotional or physical climate of a group. In a group where the atmosphere is a controlling, rigid, punishing one, the group's behavior will tend to become dependent, conforming, or apathetic.

The physical arrangements of the room also have implications for the climate of the group. If a meeting is held in a damp, cold basement with a haphazard arrangement of chairs and tables (meetings have been known to take place under such circumstances), it will require real dedication for the group to function at all. A physical environment like that is depressing. Seating arrangements are of importance because they affect the quality of communication.

Those who have studied these matters say that to have group members sit in rows slows down communication. Persons who cannot see who is speaking, to say nothing of getting the "feeling strands" in communication, or who are simply not able to hear, do not get what is being said. One of the principles of good communication is to arrange the chairs in a loose circle so that no members are out of the line of vision of the leader, and if possible the members should be able to see each other. If facilities are available they may find it more convenient to sit around a table. Ideally, someone looking in on the group should not be able to pick out the leader from his position in the group.

The leader's relation to the group probably has more effect on the group's atmosphere than any other single factor. To a large extent the leader determines by the ways he handles the meeting whether it will be formal or informal, friendly or unfriendly, rigid or permissive, judgmental or accepting.

Group atmosphere is important in any situation; but it is especially significant in a classroom where learning is supposed to take place. Teachers nowadays are being told that the emotional climate of a classroom affects learning. When, for example, a teacher is discussing an idea that challenges a position held by members of his group, he must recognize that some members need to modify attitudes, concepts, and values long associated with the old idea. They may even have strong feelings about the concept. Members of the group should feel free to question the new ideas or to express their attitudes and values. If the member feels he will be ridiculed, he will not bother to express opposition or his doubts about a new idea. What is worse a rigid atmosphere will probably help close his mind entirely against the new idea. This accents the need for a group climate that is accepting and permissive, where responses are not judged in the sense that leaders distinguish between persons and ideas expressed by persons. This, of course, is not solely the responsibility of the leader. Members too must be conscious at all times of the feelings of others and seek to be redemptive in all relationships.

The size of the group is also a contributor to threat and formality. Large groups naturally tend to get formal simply as a way of handling procedures. It is difficult to get good participation when the group exceeds 12-15 members. In groups larger than this, members may find it difficult to speak because it seems like getting up and making a speech in public, or making a motion from a conference floor! Large groups can establish better communication by breaking down into small discussion groups. A buzz group is a specialized kind of small group discussion.

Leaders Help Form Group Atmosphere

There are a number of other things a leader can do to help establish good group atmosphere. Some of these ideas were mentioned previously. They can be put to work in this context:

1. The leader should dispense with all unnecessary formality. The following are signs of formality in groups: raising hands to speak, standing to speak, addressing the chair, using titles such as Dr., Rev., Mr., or Mrs., instead of first names. How well persons in the group know each other also conditions their response. It has been observed that people who do not know the names of certain members of the group tend not to address them in discussion.

2. The leader should not downgrade ideas expressed by members of the group. At times this may be difficult. If the leader frowns disapprovingly when an idea is introduced, it will not be long until members will not feel free to say what they really mean. If they say anything at all, they will say what is expected. It always seems difficult, especially in Christian groups, to be nonjudgmental in our attitudes because we feel so strongly about what we believe. Christian convictions are important. We need not compromise basic Christian convictions. However, we close all doors against the learning of new truth when we fail to see beyond the ideas a person expresses and to understand and love the person.

3. The leader should listen carefully and be able to restate accurately what a member said, remembering that often persons do not say what they really mean. He must try to put himself into the other person's "world of meaning." He should be on guard against hearing only what he wants to hear. When he does this, he will distort what was said by the speaker. This happens almost constantly among members of a group. Each person tends to be so busy thinking what he will say next that he does not hear what is being said by others.

4. He should avoid putting people "on the spot" by pushing them to participate before they are ready. He should try to convey the impression that it is "safe to be silent."

5. He should work for a feeling of equality among members. All men are equal at the foot of the cross is a sentiment frequently quoted by Christian people, but practiced rarely. Status has invaded the church too. Occasionally, when a new group of people come together, they are invited to give their names and perhaps some biographical data such as, "Tell where you are from and

what you do." Groups studying human relations under laboratory conditions almost invariably come upon this common expedient, "Tell where you are from and what you do."

Almost as often some threatened member of the group challenges this proposal. "First names, yes. But why do you want to tell who you are and what you do? Your lists of achievements, your titles of rank or office will simply inject problems of status differences into our group. If we do this some members of our group will begin thinking if not saying, 'If Dr. so and so is here, I guess I won't have much to say. They will all be talking to him anyway.' "

Later we will say more about being redemptive in a Christian community. There will be differences in position, in ability, and in achievement, but we must learn to be Christian in our relationships and listen when a Christian brother speaks.

Leaders Help People Change

The Christian teacher's responsibility is essentially that of encouraging persons to make desirable changes in their attitudes, ideas, and conduct so what they feel and think and do is in accord with the teachings of Jesus.

This helpful statement appears in a book written by Frances C. McLester. "With loving respect for personality, Jesus appreciated all persons as they were at the moment. Having a deep-rooted belief in the possibilities of human beings, He could look beyond their present state of achievement to what they were capable of becoming. For example, He saw in the fickle and wavering Peter the roots of strong and steadfast qualities. So He gave special guidance to this Cephas, or 'rock,' who later developed the faith in Christ that is the foundation of the life of the Christian church and all its members.

"We humbly acknowledge that in even the best of us the achievement of Christian character is never fully realized. Rather, it is a continuing process that demands reliance on God and His grace and unflagging effort on our part. Like Paul, we press on toward the goal that is before us. None of us has reached the point where he no longer needs to change to improve the quality of his living. Each individual should be on a continual quest to discover what it means to be Christian in all sorts of situations and in relation to all sorts of persons. And it is our purpose as teachers not only to seek God and His righteousness ourselves, but also to lead others to do so."[1]

Teaching in its simplest definition is helping persons make desirable changes. Actually neither you nor I can make changes in anyone. In the matter of Christian growth, only God can change persons. But helping a person change is often a difficult and complicated task. Perhaps in the church we have too often oversimplified the matter by thinking all we have to do is to pipe out the information and, presto, people will change! What we see in our churches is evidence that many desired changes have not taken place. Our task is the delicate and intricate one of helping persons open their lives to the guidance of the Holy Spirit and become Christian. We cannot do this through coercion; each person must make his own response. When we have done the best we can, the test of the adequacy of our teaching is not what we know or have done, but whether changes have taken place in the persons taught.

Groups as a Means of Change

As frequently pointed out in these pages, each individual associates not only with other individuals, but also with groups of many kinds. Most teaching situations in the church occur in small groups. Recent research of social scientists reveals some exciting things about influence of groups as a medium of change.

They remind us that we who work in the church may have overlooked the power of a group to bring changes in people. We learn most readily by being together, provided the right conditions prevail. When we stop to think of it, our behavior, our attitudes, and values are all firmly grounded in the groups to which we belong. We learn to live together by being together. The church has always known the power of Christian fellowship, but it has not always made practical use of this knowledge. There are more than pious, church attendance building reasons for insisting that Christians should be vitally related to church groups.

The church has had its groups of children and adults, but too often these were looked upon as a collection of individuals. In the interest of economy a teacher was secured to pour information into a dozen individual heads. All the while, teachers have been missing the creative possibilities untapped in the group before them!

Can one speak of a Sunday-school class as a group? It is true that not everyone in the class comes of his own accord. Some are pushed, some are cajoled, some are indifferent, and others come gladly. Nevertheless, a Sunday-school class does fulfill some basic requirements of a group. It is a gathering of persons, meeting regularly, much the same persons at every meeting, sharing common goals, doing better together than any member could do alone, gradually influencing each other, stimulating each other through discussion and developing plans impossible alone, and as a result learning more and better than they would alone.

A church group like any other group may function as a medium of change. There are at least three ways in which the group acts as a medium of change:

1. The more attractive the group is to the member, the greater the influence the group can exert on its members. It has been shown by research that in more cohesive groups (groups that stick together well) there is greater readiness of members to try to influence others. There is also more readiness to be influenced by others. For those who wish to apply this principle the practical problem is how to make church groups more attractive to members.

Applying this principle to the classroom Leland P. Bradford writing about "Group Forces Affecting Learning" says,

"The desirability of the group largely determines the degree of influence it has upon the individual member. If the group is prevented from consciously forming as a group; if individual relations are set between teacher and pupil and not among pupils; and if no group goal or product is possible, forces of group belongingness and pride leading toward cohesiveness are inhibited. If present, they have arisen because the group coalesced in a resistance to teacher and learning activities, and in this case group cohesive forces serve to inhibit learning."[2] He is simply saying that failure to help members of the class become a smoothly functioning group cuts down what they are able to learn.

2. Where there is a strong sense of loyalty to a group, it will exert forces for change on the member. The frequent gap between teacher and student, doctor and patient, preacher and church member can be a real obstacle to acceptance of new ways of living. Here we are speaking about the degree of identification a member feels for the group. Does he feel he really belongs? Is this the kind of group where he feels at home and where he likes to be? The practical questions for church workers dealing with groups include: How can we help members identify? How can we close the gap between teacher and student? How can we help group members feel comfortable in each other's company?

There are studies which show that more learning results from discussion in which members of a class participated freely under good leadership than from a lecture.

Discussion has the function of securing member participation. Moreover, people learn certain things better through discussion than by the lecture method. Frank Cheavens says, "From the point of view of factual learning (acquiring information which may later be tested objectively as in an examination) the lecture method is as effective as discussion. There are enough experimental studies to demonstrate that the two methods are about equally productive. However, a sharp distinction should be made between the learning which results in remembering facts and the learning which results in changes in behavior. The discussion method appears to be more efficient in the latter type of learning. Factual learning is important and valuable. This should not ever be minimized. When most people think of learning, this is their concept. . . . Group members having gone through a good discussion may also expect certain, definite, factual knowledge. . . . Over and beyond the factual knowledge, and more important from the standpoint of mental health, are the new skills in human relations resulting from participating in free discussion."[3]

3. In the Christian context, the group will have increasing influence with the member as he accepts its beliefs and values.

William G. Dyer holds that "nearly all persons observe that as they move from one situation or set of relationships to another their behavior changes. One does not behave the same way in church as he does at work, at home, at a party. . . . Each situation demands some different responses which most people assume.

"It should be recognized that most people 'internalize' the demands of the role. . . . In order to maintain his self-respect, his respect from others, his feelings of adequacy and self-worth, the individual 'needs' to perform those roles he has accepted."[4] The member tends to feel committed to decisions and goals if he has helped to make them.

Groups May Become a Redemptive Fellowship

Up to this point we have discussed how we might help to create a group atmosphere which would help everyone participate. In the remaining section we must say something about our Christian responsibility for fostering a community of love, acceptance, and concern. How can we make the relationships with persons in groups the redemptive Christian fellowship it ought to be?

Everyone reading this section ought also to read the book, *Life Together,* by Dietrich Bonhoeffer. Realizing this may be an impossible ideal, there will be rather extensive quotes from the book.

Bonhoeffer wrote the book mentioned above out of his own experience of the deep meaning of Christian community found in life together in an "underground" seminary established by the confessing church in Germany under Hitler. He forcibly makes the point with which we begin here that because of what Christ has done for the Christian in saving him from sin and raising him to newness of life, *he needs to live this new life in a community of fellowship with fellow Christians.*

Hear what Bonhoeffer says about the Christian's need for his brother. Life would be incomplete without him. "It is true, of course, that what is an unspeakable gift of God for the lonely individual is easily disregarded and trodden under foot by those who have the gift every day. It is easily forgotten that the fellowship of Christian brethren is a gift of grace, a gift of the kingdom of God that any day may be taken from us, that the time that still separates us from utter loneliness may be brief indeed. Therefore, let him who until now has had the privilege of living a common Christian life with other Christians praise God's grace from the bottom of his heart. Let him thank God on his knees and declare: It is grace, nothing but grace that we are allowed to live in community with Christian brethren."[5]

About the love and concern that ought to be expressed in the Christian community Bonhoeffer writes, "But God has put this Word into the mouth of men in order that it may be communicated to other men. When one person is struck by the Word, he speaks it to others. God has willed that we should seek and find His living Word in the witness of a brother, in the mouth of man. Therefore, the Christian needs another Christian who speaks God's Word to him. He needs him again and again when he becomes uncertain and discouraged. . . . But without Christ we also would not know our brother, nor could we come to him. The way is blocked by our own ego. Christ opened up the way to God and to our brother."[6]

What is our obligation to selfish, insincere, hypocritical, domineering, status-seeking persons who so often complicate our group relations? Do Christians act in such ways? Reluctantly we will have to admit they do. Is there a redemptive way to deal with such persons? We believe there is. The place to begin is to acknowledge that some of these traits—and many more—are found in each of us. "We thank God for giving us brethren who live by His call, by His forgiveness, and His promise. We do not complain of what God does not give us; we rather thank God for what He does give us daily. And is not what has been given us enough: brothers, who will go on living with us through sin and need under the blessing of His grace? Is the divine gift of Christian fellowship anything less than this, any day, even the most difficult and distressing day? Even when sin and misunderstanding burden the communal life, is not the sinning brother still a brother, with whom I, too, stand under the Word of Christ? Will not his sin be a constant occasion for me to give thanks that both of us may live in the forgiving love of God in Jesus Christ?"[7]

Are we able to love other persons in a mature way? Are we free to let the other person be what God intended him to be? This we can learn through the tensions of Christian community. "Human love is directed to the other person for his own sake, spiritual love loves him for Christ's sake. . . . Human love desires the other person, his company, his answering love, but it does not serve him. On the contrary, it continues to desire even when it seems to be serving. . . . Human love is by its very nature desire—desire for human community. So long as it can satisfy this desire in some way, it will not give it up, even for the sake of truth, even for the sake of genuine love for others. But where it can no longer expect its desire to be fulfilled, there it stops short—namely, in the face of an enemy. There it turns into hatred, contempt, and calumny."[8]

"This means that I must release the other person from every attempt of mine to regulate, coerce, and dominate him with my love. The other person needs to retain his independence of me, to be loved for what he is, as one for whom Christ became man, died, and rose again, for whom Christ brought forgiveness of sins and eternal life. Because Christ has long since acted decisively for my brother, before I could begin to act, I must leave him his freedom to be Christ's; I must meet him only as the person that he already is in Christ's eyes."[9]

"The exclusion of the weak and insignificant, the seemingly useless people, from a Christian community may actually mean the exclusion of Christ; in the poor brother Christ is knocking at the door. We must therefore be very careful at this point."[10]

A Christian group should be a community of love, acceptance, and concern. Without Christ a redemptive fellowship is impossible, without Christ we would be estranged from our brother and be bound by our own egos. The sinning brother is still a brother. In the Christian fellowship we all stand in need of the forgiving love of God. Are we able to let the other person be what God intended him to be without trying to dominate, coerce, or regulate him with our love? In our associations with other persons in a group we may learn again the meaning of redemption.

1. Frances C. McLester, *Teaching in the Church School* (Nashville: Abingdon Press, 1961), pp. 12, 13.

2. From *Journal of the National Association of Women Deans and Counselors,* Vol. 23, No. 3 (April 1960).

3. Frank Cheavens, *Leading Group Discussions* (The University of Texas, Austin 12, Texas, 1958).

4. William C. Dyer, from an article "Looking at Conflict," reprinted from *Adult Leadership.*

5. Dietrich Bonhoeffer, *Life Together* (New York: Harper and Brothers, 1954), p. 20.

6. *Ibid.,* pp. 22, 23.

7. *Ibid.,* p. 28.

8. *Ibid.,* p. 34.

9. *Ibid.,* pp. 35, 36.

10. *Ibid.,* p. 38.

Chapter 8

Making up Our Minds—Together

Leaders working with groups in the church need to examine carefully the process of decision-making. People come together for a variety of purposes, sometimes for fellowship, sometimes to make decisions about important matters. A planning committee usually comes together to reach a decision or solve a problem. All of us have been in groups that floundered in making decisions. Leaders sometimes experience frustration in trying to get an effective vote or consensus. One of the skills leaders need is to improve the decision-making process.

Decision-making in groups can be improved by learning to follow the logical steps of the decision-making process. These steps are not always followed in logical order but all must be included if effective action is to result.

Decision-making is a more complex process than is commonly recognized. While the gathering of facts and improvement of individual skills are important, these are secondary to an understanding of what really takes place in the group. Decision-making is a process in which many persons in the group exert influence in a variety of ways. Decision-making and decision-implementation are basically inseparable.

Understood in this way, decision-making has no precise beginning or ending. As long as action is required the decision is never complete. It can be appealed, revised, or even reversed.

Thus if we want to understand the process of decision-making, we must understand *all* of it.

The leader who is concerned with improving the process of decision-making will give serious thought to the way in which most decisions are actually made, and will try to improve the decisions and their carrying out by helping others to help each other. The virtue of shared decision-making responsibility is that people generally support what they help to create.

Wrong Ideas About Decision-Making

If the description of the decision-making process given above is correct, then there are misconceptions about decision-making prevalent in the church as they are elsewhere. One such mistaken notion is that only the designated leader makes decisions. Those who take this approach would concern themselves with improving the capability of the individual administrator or leader for making good decisions. Those who hold this view would say the job of the leader is to hand down decisions. Recent research has demonstrated that people at all levels in an organization make decisions. The decisions are by no means all made by leaders of the organization. Take a religious bookstore for an example. Clerks who work there make decisions about the kind of books to be sold, the kind of service the store will provide. How the janitor cleans the store has implications for sales; all these decisions not made by leaders in the organization nevertheless affect the organization.

It is assumed that most persons reading this manual are engaged in the work of the church, functioning in leadership positions. How impossible it is, for example, for the pastor or the superintendent to hand down a decision can be seen in the following illustration. The superintendent has called a meeting in which he is pressing for a decision to make his Sunday school a friendly inviting school. Whether or not his group succeeds in making the decision to be friendly will be affected in large measure by the way individual members express friendliness; if they do not speak to strangers at the door, or if classes fail to have an inviting atmosphere that takes people in and makes them part of the fellowship; if in the larger fellowship people do not know each other and make no effort to learn to know each other the superintendent's plans will fail. Vital decisions are being made at other levels which will affect the decision the superintendent is pressing for in this meeting.

Another mistaken notion about decision-making is that decisions can be separated from implementation. When a decision-making body fails to keep in mind who is going to carry out the proposed action and how willingly it will be done, it is overlooking a rather crucial aspect of decision-making. There is no point in making a decision that cannot be carried out. Go back to the illustration above. If the superintendent's decision is forced on the group, things will remain pretty much as they were. But if members of the group really get concerned and participate in making the decision, things will begin to change.

Still another fallacy about decision-making is the idea that decision-making always involves some kind of action. Frequently frustrated committees take no action, thinking that thereby they bypass responsibility for making a decision. Actually they made a decision. In reality decisions occur by doing nothing. Too many decisions in the work of the church are made in that way. An administrator once said jokingly, if you leave an unanswered letter on your desk long enough, it will answer itself. He was right, but this is not the way to answer letters or make decisions.

Good information will not necessarily insure a good decision. People do not always act responsibly in the light of facts. A large amount of information is not always an indication of the right kind.

Conditions That Improve Decision-Making

Before analyzing further the steps involved in decision-making, it will be helpful to look at some of the conditions that facilitate the process of decision-making. One such condition is that the group be qualified to make the decision.

The difficulty of making decisions stick should be kept in mind when decisions are made. People tend to carry out decisions which they helped to formulate. Therefore, leaders will be wise to include in the process of decision-making persons who will ultimately be responsible for implementing it.

The decision-making process will be improved where members have learned to work together effectively as a group. By this time it should be clear that group action is a complex thing. Decision-making is a difficult process at best. It depends upon the kind of working relationships in which disagreement, creativity, and shared responsibility can work without hindrance.

A group's effectiveness in decision-making depends also on the use of proper procedures. Shall parliamentary procedures be used? Perhaps in a large body the only feasible procedure is to decide issues by voting. A large body may develop some procedures such as deciding issues by the majority or two thirds rule. Frequently, however, votes tend to polarize groups. They create minority groups which result in problems later on.

In recent years there have been many attempts to get away from vote taking. Some leaders have gone so far as to try for unanimous decisions. As a rule, human nature being what it is, this is extremely unlikely in the process of decision-making.

Christian groups will do well to work toward getting consensus rather than to take votes. According to Franklin H. Littell, the early Anabaptist practice of working for consensus is part of the heritage the free church left to democracy in our day.

Writing about the meaning of consensus Gordon Lippitt says, "It is the opinion of this author that there is a difference between unanimous decision-making and a 'consensus decision.' In a consensus type of decision, the members of the group agree on the next steps, but those who are not in agreement with the decision reserve the right to have the tentative decision tested and evaluated for later assessment. In other words, certain members of the group will agree that on a 'provisional try' or a 'first time' basis we could try out a particular alternative; but they want to put in certain evaluative means for testing whether or not the feelings of the majority are the most appropriate for group action. In a very real sense, this is different from compromise. In a compromise situation, the decision is taken from two opposing points of view and becomes something quite different from either of them. In the consensus type of decision, individuals in the group might be saying that they are 'not sure' of the best decision, but realizing the need for action, they will build in some committment to an action step that will be assessed later."[1]

Steps in Decision-Making

Following are the steps in the decision-making process. If it is true that group after group has difficulty making decisions, a clear understanding of what is involved in decision-making should help avoid some of the pitfalls.

1. The group should work for a clear definition of the problem. What is expected? What specifically is needed? What quality or type of pattern?What quantity? What are the time factors? The priorities? Can we afford it? What procedures or methods are desirable? Who will do what? Do they understand this when they agree? Will this decision fit the policy of the larger organization?

If the problem the group is trying to solve is unclear, much of the group's time will be wasted. What is worse, frustrations and tensions will build up. In some cases the assignment coming to a group may be so vague or ambiguous that the group cannot come to grips with it. It has frequently been demonstrated in role playing that groups working with an ambiguous assignment build up tensions and even hostility.

Take this situation as an illustration of the kind of problem the church group might be called upon to deal with. A committee is appointed to study and make a recommendation on how to correlate the Christian activities in the congregation. This is a general assignment. First the committee must determine what its specific task is. It knows for example that there is a Sunday-school committee and a committee on Christian education which have overlapping interests. The committee may recommend that there be one over-all Christian education committee, or it may recommend that the job is too big for one committee. The problem will require study. Facts must be gathered and finally a recommendation must be made to the parent group. The specific problem in this case is: Shall we recommend one over-all Christian education committee?

2. The second step in the process of decision-making is suggesting alternatives. As many reasonable solutions as possible should be worked out as the time and circumstances permit. All

members of the group ought to participate in this discussion. This tentative exploration for solutions may indicate areas in which further information is needed. If a decision is not pressing, the group may postpone the decision to a later time when the needed information will be available.

3. The next step is weighing the alternatives. In this step the group must envision what might be the result if the action were taken. What would be the consequences of taking this action? In terms of the committee problem just referred to, what would be the wisest course of action? Would the wisest course be to continue to have two separate committees—one working separately on Sunday-school matters, the other on remaining Christian education activities?

Another aspect of weighing the alternatives is to evaluate the proposed action in the light of consequences. What jobs will need to be filled if the decision is put into action? In terms of the illustration referred to above, if there were to be one general Christian education committee, could it handle all Christian education activities—the Sunday school, vacation Bible school, boys' clubs, girls' clubs, midweek services, Sunday night programs, etc. Would it need subcommittees in order to function properly, and if so, would the church be any better off than it is now in having two committees?

Perhaps an entirely different illustration will set the issue in sharper focus. Suppose a curriculum committee of a Sunday school of a hundred members is ready to propose a *closely graded* Sunday-school curriculum for use in its school. Weighing the consequences of this proposed action would mean that the committee must deal with the question of who will teach this curriculum if it is adopted. It may mean that a Sunday school this size cannot produce enough trained teachers to use a curriculum designed for each grade in addition to the youth and adult classes. As a result of exploring the alternatives, it becomes clear this is not a feasible action.

4. The next step is making the decision. There are always some people who have little respect for or appreciation for the decisions made by a committee. One such person once said a camel is a horse put together by a committee.

Herbert Bonner in his book, *Group Dynamics, Principles and Applications,* states that on the basis of present research one thing is clear, viz., that the traditional contempt for the ability of a group to direct its own activities and solve its problems collectively is wholly unjustified.

This is, so he says, because in many problem situations the individual cannot bring the large variety of skills needed.

A single individual does not possess sufficient skills and wisdom to face every task productively. Researches have shown that productive interaction among members of a group diminish as the group becomes either too large or too small.

In the process of making its decision the group should work toward arriving at consensus rather than to push through an action by vote taking. Arriving at a consensus is much more difficult and more time consuming than vote taking, but in a Christian brotherhood where relationships to other persons are important, the extra effort will be justified.

5. After the decision has been made, plans for action need to be laid out. Suppose a committee has just decided to have a training institute for summer Bible school teachers. If this action is to succeed other plans must be completed. Who will be the leaders for this training institute? Who will notify them? Does the committee have sufficient funds to carry out the project? Who will handle the promotion for the institute? What facilities are available for a meeting place? for meals? for lodging? for transportation? This is what it might mean to follow through on a decision to have a training institute for teachers.

6. Scheduling is another part of the decision-making process. Applied to the illustration above, when will the teachers institute be held? Who will do what when?

7. Finally, the group should evaluate its action. If the group follows through the complete cycle of decision-making it will evaluate its action after a period of time to determine whether the plan and the decision were successful. Careful, thoughtful evaluation should enable the group to make better decisions next time.

Some Blocks to Decision-Making

There are a variety of reasons why groups are sometimes unable to make decisions. In the section that follows we will try to identify some blocks to effective decision-making.

1. One block is the assumption that the problem confronting the group is clear. But it may not be clear. Realizing that persons come into a group with differing backgrounds and differing understandings, we can easily imagine that a problem means different things to different people. For a group to function effectively in the decision-making process, there must not only be a basic problem of interest and importance to the group that is meeting to discuss it, but that problem should be clear. During this class session you may be given an opportunity to observe a role play in which a group is given an ambiguous assignment to see what happens. If there are indications a problem is not clear, time should be taken to clarify what kind of decision the group is being called upon to make.

2. Another difficulty in some groups is the element of threat. Members are not sure they are completely free to participate in a decision because of possible consequences outside the group. Perhaps the parent organization which appointed the committee will not be inclined to receive the proposed action favorably. Or there may be in the working group itself an influential member who has status in the community and equally strong views on the subject being discussed. Weaker members of the group may not feel free to oppose him.

3. Again discussion, particularly in an immature group, may have "polarized" members. It happens not infrequently that during a strong argument which reaches emotional levels members tend to take sides on opposite "poles" of the question. This is why attention to group maintenance roles is important at all times. Good interpersonal relations and a common understanding among group members will be effective in reducing polarization (the taking of sides) and ensuing hostility among members.

4. Formalism is a block to effective group action. Groups in which members do not feel free to express real concerns will have difficulty coming to a decision. Indications of formality are

addressing the chair as Mr. Chairman, referring to members of the group as Mr., Rev., or Dr., the making of formal motions which require vote taking.

5. Lack of information or inexperience may block the progress of a group to say nothing of making a good decision. As indicated above, decision-making requires flexibility in performing group member roles. Group maintenance is especially important in the process of decision-making. It is unfortunate that groups sometimes insist on trying to make decisions without adequate information. Occasionally they do not recognize that the real problem is lack of information. In such cases a member should ask: Do we have the necessary information today to make this decision? If the decision isn't made in the light of facts besides the damage done, if it was the wrong decision, it will have to be revised or made again later.

6. Occasionally a good decision is made impossible by premature voting. An old parliamentary trick observed in many groups is to bring a question to a vote before there is adequate time for opposition to it. Instead of pushing through the action intended, it frequently results in a wrong decision—if a decision is reached at all. Forcing the hand of a group creates more problems than it solves.

7. Scapegoating is another device used to avoid decision-making. When a group fails to carry out its task, it is said to be "taking flight" from its task. Instead of discussing the problem at hand members of the group may swap stories, argue over trivial details, take "coke breaks," or even take long excursions from the task before it. One explanation of why groups do not stay on the subject at hand is that they find it much more to their liking to discuss something else. The group may even find it distasteful to carry out an assignment.

8. Procedural maneuvers may also block decision-making. A common one is to postpone an action. Another is to decide that the responsibility belongs to another group or another individual. It is not uncommon even in the church to find a task bandied about from group to group and in the end being done by no one.

Techniques for Mobilizing Group Resources

Here are some methods which will help to get the decision-making process started or restarted when the group is stalled.

1. *Discussion.* Discussion is one method a group can use in the process of decision-making. It permits the group to explore all sides of a question. Each member around the table differs from every other member, not only in physical appearance but also in skills, education, training, and experience. Each person looks at the problem from the perspective of his interest and his own frame of reference and outlook. In the wide differences expressed, the mature group will find the varied resources necessary to explore a problem.

Discussion is a useful way of bringing views and opinions to correction and criticism. Honest discussion opens up minds to new ideas. New facts and points of view can set wrong ideas right. The give and take of exploring ideas helps to create a climate in which decisions made will be more readily accepted. Discussion permits clarification, challenge, correction, modification, assimilation, and appreciation.

2. *Role playing.* Role playing is another method used to introduce ideas, points of view, or emotional feelings into a discussion. Basically, it is an unrehearsed acting out of situations which confront the members of a group. In role playing members feel free to portray life situations without the punishments that might occur in real life. Role playing is a useful technique to help the decision-making process focus a specific problem so that members have a common situation to face. It may be used to test out alternative ways of dealing with the problems at hand, or to develop a more sensitive awareness of the issues at hand. It may even be used to work through difficulties the group itself encountered in working on the problem.

3. *Buzz sessions.* In spite of the fact that buzz sessions have been abused, they serve a useful purpose. A technique is useful only insofar as it helps a group produce. Usually a buzz group includes about six members. It may meet for five or six minutes. Thelen suggests four uses of the buzz group: (a) to get the discussion going on significant problems; (b) to set up an agenda for

meaningful learning experience; (c) to counteract the feeling of apathy and to redirect the group toward action; (d) to test a set of ideas and to increase communication between speaker and audience.

4. *Brainstorming.* Brainstorming is a method used to get as many ideas out into the open as possible. A usual stipulation is that no idea shall be thrown out as ridiculous. Usually a member of the group records all the ideas given. It is hoped that from this list of new ideas may come the clues to the solution of the problem being discussed.

Decision-Making Model

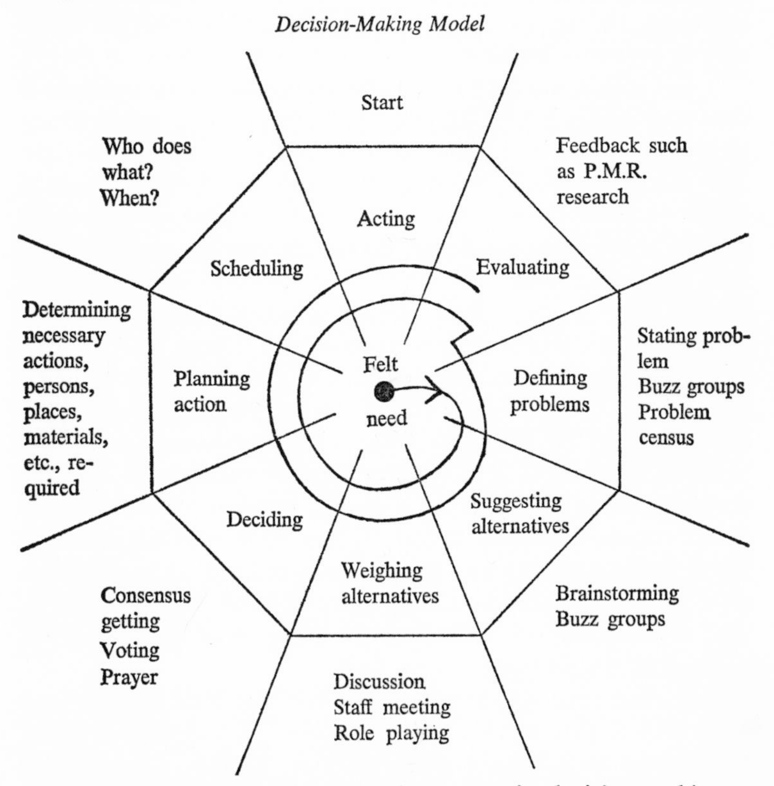

The inner octagonal spaces show steps in decision-making.

The outer octagonal spaces show methods appropriate to each step.

5. *Silence.* A period of silence may be used effectively when the group process bogs down. The Friends have traditionally made good use of consensus and periods of silence. John R. Mott used to say when a group failed to produce, "Brethren, we are getting nowhere. At such points when we were apt to flounder and get on one another's nerves as a substitute for getting ahead with the work at hand, I have recess meetings for intercession and meditation. During the recess the group members relax, gather in natural huddles, and return with clarified points of view and readiness to get on with the work again."[2]

1. Gordon L. Lippitt, "Improving Decision-Making with Groups." Article originally appeared in *Youth Work with Youth* (April 1958), published by National Board of YMCA.

2. John R. Mott, quoted in *The Group Workshop Way in the Church,* Paul F. Douglass (New York: Association Press, 1956), p. 106.

3. Chart designed by David Wieand on basis of materials from various resources.

Chapter 9

Setting Goals and Evaluating Results

Have you ever belonged to an organization which seemed to exist because it always existed? which seems to keep on going because people keep on coming to the meetings? That kind of an organization might even be found in a church. Sometimes meetings seem to be held for their own sake.

What are the telltale clues to membership behavior in an organization that seems to have lost its purpose? Attendance is emphasized, time is taken for setting up agendas, considerable time is spent in reading formal minutes where minutes are kept. Attention is given to the order of business, but the real function of the organization may be buried in the maze of organizational procedure and tradition. This may be true of a college class, a PTA, or even an organization within the church.

Goal Setting

A mature group accepts as one of its first responsibilities the clarification of its goals. Every group is working toward some kind of goal, even though it may be unclear or unstated. The goal may be recreation, it may be the study of problems, it may be the discussion of books, it may be protection against a real or imagined danger, or it may be to listen to a program.

Those of us who belong to groups might well ask ourselves the following questions: Why do I attend this meeting? How does it serve my needs? If it were discontinued, would it be missed?

The problem facing any group is to weld a variety of individual goals into a realistic goal which can be adopted by the group. This process becomes difficult because individuals come into the group with diverse purposes. The point was made in a previous session that individuals come into a group with backgrounds of "different private worlds." Each person coming to the same meeting will have his own individualized expectations for that meeting, his own conviction about what ought to be done. Sometimes an individual will believe he is right and everyone else is wrong. Or he may have no strong ideas at all and eagerly seek someone to tell him what to think and do.

Consequently, one of the things we must recognize, especially in the early stages of group development, is that persons come into a group with different expectations. It is possible that a mother may go to a meeting to get away from household duties. A family may go to a conference for a holiday. A student may be taking the course to fulfill a graduation requirement. A businessman may attend a community meeting because "it raises his status." Persons are sometimes found in church groups who are there because it's the proper thing to do. They may not be there because of conviction.

A new group needs to formulate a satisfactory statement of its goals. Even after the group has been together for a time, it should periodically re-examine its goals. If group members are to continue to maintain a satisfactory relation to the group, they must be able to identify with the things the group proposes to do. If the purpose of the group is to meet to review books and a group member dislikes reading, the likelihood is he will find it difficult to relate to the group. The individual member must have the feeling that the goals of the group are *his* goals and that the group is *his* group, and its decisions are *his* decisions because he participated in making them.

Group Goals and Church Workers

A discussion of group goals may at first sight seem far removed from the usual activities of church workers. But are they really? Take the typical problems encountered by teachers, for example. Is it not true that many of the frustrations encountered by teachers can be traced to a simple cause like lack of goal clarity? What is the teacher really trying to do? Can he simply tell the class, "This is what we are going to do," and expect that all the members of the class will come along? Can he assume that all the members of his class want to do what he wants to do? There are limitations to this to be sure. If the teacher is appointed to teach a Bible course, the Bible course should be taught. But there are a variety of ways in which Bible courses may be taught. What part of the Bible would be most significant for the age group? How does one relate what is being learned about the Bible to the experience of members in the group? How does the Bible come alive in the twentieth century?

Consider these case studies from a church school situation to demonstrate what happens when teachers dominate the group by ignoring goal formation by the group. Mrs. M. S. had an alert group of ten juniors in church school. She had made good plans for use of the curriculum materials provided on the missionary outreach of the church in Africa. Her story material was interesting and she was "well prepared." When the boys and girls saw the pictures of Congolese, they were reminded of the news reports of difficulties between races in the United States. Several tried to introduce their concern. Each time the teacher said, "Isn't that too bad!" and then quickly got back to her subject, the Congo. Two children who had tried to introduce these things that concerned them became apathetic and seemed to be in a daydreaming mood.

A primary department superintendent was trying to decide on a Christmas project with her children. She had asked them to make suggestions and they were responding well. She kept saying, "Is there something else you have forgotten?" They kept producing and finally she said, "Nobody has thought of sending gifts to our Navaho mission. Wouldn't that be a good thing to do?" No response except from one child who could always be depended on to agree with the superintendent. She went on, "I think that would be a good thing to do. Let's try to think between now and next Sunday what we could do for the Navahos." This teacher resisted member contributions toward group goal formation. She didn't seem to realize that the children would be much more interested in working toward a project they had helped to decide, rather than to have one imposed on them. This discussion was merely a disguise for the teacher to impose her will on children.[1]

In the work of the church designated leaders may pay too little attention to goal formation by members of the group. Because it's a church group it is assumed everyone comes with the same purpose. This is not necessarily so. No leader can presume to set a goal for a group. When this happens, the goal does not belong to members of the group and consequently the activity will not challenge their full co-operation.

A group goal cannot be decided upon until after the group has had an opportunity to help shape it. It may be expected that not everyone will be completely satisfied with it, but if each member has an opportunity to help formulate the goal, there is a better chance of his making it his own. One way of helping the group adopt a goal is to ask each member what he thinks they should do. His presence in the group would suggest that he hopes to get something out of it. The ideas suggested should be pooled. No idea should be ignored or shut off. If possible, consensus should be reached. The group goal is the "new thing" that has emerged from sharing and pooling of ideas.

Characteristics of Good Goals

It may be helpful in this connection to point out some characteristics of good goals.

1. The goal should be attainable. The degree of difficulty standing between the present and the attainment of the goal affect the value of the goal to the individual. The goal should be realistic in relation to the resources of the group.

2. The goal should be clearly understood by all. This may mean, as pointed out above, that a group should spend time clarifying what its goals are.

3. Opportunity should be given for members of the group to share in the formulation of the group goals.

4. Subgoals should be related to the group goals. Groups may have short term or long-range goals.

5. Group goals should be flexible too. Sometimes a goal previously set no longer serves the needs of the group. Mature groups learn to redefine or change the goals when necessary. Recognizing when the goal is no longer appropriate is an important skill for a group to learn.

An important question for group members to ask is: Have I helped responsibly to set the group's goal? It is a display of poor Christian grace to sit back and complain about what a group is doing if we haven't made an honest attempt to help direct its activity.

Why Evaluate?

In addition to formulating clear goals, a mature group evaluates its activities in the light of its goals. Two teachers coming home from a PTA meeting were asked, "What did you think of the meeting?" Miss Flynn replied, "Oh, it was the usual thing. We got out about ten o'clock. It was a fairly good meeting." Miss Smucker described the meeting in a different way. She looked beneath the surface. "There were some things that made me wonder about last night's meeting. For one thing, we began 20 minutes late. The committee reports were dry and not what the group expected, and one report was missing. During the time that was left two members argued about the wording of a resolution concerning a bloodmobile that was to be sent to the churches. It really wasn't important, but it seemed neither of them could back down and they took a lot of our time. During that deadlock I noticed quite a number of people were looking at their watches."

These two reports about a meeting suggest some important things about people's ability to evaluate what is happening in a group. Mature group members should become sensitive to what is happening in a group and be able to evaluate group process.

What to Evaluate

Group process refers to the way groups function. Here we are discussing the evaluation of group process. A group may be either healthy or sick, mature or immature. Following are the kind of questions that can be asked about group process. 1. How many of the members were *really* involved in the discussion? 2. How well is the group using its resources? 3. How does the group make decisions? Does it assign work that is not a concern to the whole group to subcommittees? How long does it take a group to make a simple decision? 4. Do the same subjects keep coming up for discussion even though they have supposedly been "settled"? 5. Do the members really understand one another's ideas, plans, or proposals? 6. Do members respond by making evaluative judgments—"this is bad" or "this is wonderful"? Did they pass judgment on ideas before they clearly understand them? 7. Are some persons always getting recognition, while others are ignored? If things go wrong, is there a tendency to fix the blame on a certain subgroup rather than accepting it by the group as a whole?[2] 8. How much does the group depend on the designated leader?

If it is important for a group to set clearly defined goals, then it is equally important for the group to evaluate whether these goals are being met. A healthy group must determine whether the activities it is engaging in are what the group wants—that is, whether or not the group goals are being met or whether the group would like to try other activities. Continual evaluation is important to the growth of the group.

When observers or members of the group make evaluations about group process, they should try to be positive. The observer tries to be objective in presenting his observations. He tries to distinguish between what is objectively a fact and what may be personal feeling or an interpretation of the facts. He would be well advised to use phrases like this. "I wonder if . . ." or "It seems to me . . ." or "I'd like to have you check me on this." An observer appointed to watch the operations of the group tries to answer questions like these. 1. Are our meetings getting the job done? That is, are they reaching the goal? 2. Is our group making progress, or is it always getting "bogged down." 3. Are the potential abilities of group members being used? or are we ignoring resources? 4. Are members of the group working well together?

Wherever people come together, critical evaluations will be made, whether or not there is opportunity to express them. These criticisms, if properly used, could become useful. We have all been in situations in which the only course open to members was to express suggestions about a group situation to persons sitting nearby or to share feelings with friends or members of the family after the meeting. Often suggestions are not made at all because of fear of offending friends or the feeling that suggestions would not be followed anyway.

Sometimes groups appoint a perceptive group member to observe or evaluate and report back later. This report serves as a kind of mirror in which the group can see its activities and get back on the track.

For instance, an observer might keep a participation diagram and by showing it to the group reveal the fact that a few members talk quite often while some members did not talk at all. Why? Quite often when a group meets for the first time the least bit of humor will bring laughter. If at the conclusion of a meeting, an observer were asked to make a report he might ask, among other things, "Was the boisterous laughter a cover for feelings of insecurity in a new situation?"

How to Evaluate

The attainment of goals may at times be difficult to evaluate. For instance, a church group might have as its goal "learning to better understand the Negro in our city." The problem of measuring improvement in understanding is difficult. Perhaps the best the group can do is to make some estimate or simply ask members.

There are a number of ways to make evaluations. We have already mentioned some. They may be verbal, written, formal or informal, or the result of a detailed study. Frequently group members make evaluations by expressing an opinion, making a statement of aims, or giving a summary.

One form of written evaluation is the well-known post meeting reaction sheet (PMR). (A sample appears at the end of this chapter.) It is a small piece of paper with not more than four or five questions requiring brief answers.

To summarize ways of evaluation:

1. Group members themselves help with evaluation.

2. The group may formally appoint an observer to evaluate its progress.

3. Post meeting evaluation sheets may be filled out after the meeting. Post meeting reaction sheets take only a minute or two to fill out. They help the designated leader and group members find out whether the group is getting what it wants.

Areas Requiring Continuous Evaluation

It may seem for church workers at least that we have become lost in technicalities. If it needs to be said again—our relation to other persons is a matter of serious Christian concern. There are at least five areas for which continuous evaluation is needed. They are needed no less for teachers and church workers than for others.

1. *How did the leader behave?*

(1) Was leadership distributed among group members?

(2) Were there "status struggles" in the group? In other words, were several or more members in the group struggling for leadership?

(3) Was there a power structure or hidden agenda?

(4) Was the leader autocratic? paternalistic? or democratic?

(5) What kind of control did the leader exert? (as seen in ease of movement, treatment of absentees or latecomers) What were the attitudes of the group toward leadership?

2. *What was the physical atmosphere in the group?*

(1) Were the temperature of the room and ventilation right for physical comfort?

(2) Were there proper seating arrangements, tables, ample space?

(3) Were there distractions (open doors, passers-by, etc.)?

3. *What was the emotional climate?*

(1) Was there warmth and friendliness?

(2) Spontaneity and informality?

(3) Was there a minimum amount of threat or hostility?

(4) Was the climate permissive? (Did members say what they wanted to say?)

(5) Were there tension-releasing activities in the group?

(6) Did members experience real encounter?

(7) What was the emotional tone of the discussion?

(8) Were attitudes expressed nonjudgmental?

(9) Was there sensitivity to the needs of others?

4. *What was the quality and quantity of the work accomplished?*

(1) Was the task accomplished at the expense of individual members? Was the group task oriented? Was there proper balance between task and maintenance functions?

(2) Was the group productive in terms of ideas, decisions reached, meeting its goals?

(3) Did the group wander away from the task?

(4) Was the group able to make good decisions promptly?

5. *How did members participate?*

(1) Did members listen to each other and show this by "building" on conversation?

(2) Did members make positive assertions in an antagonistic way?

(3) Was there flexibility in role distribution among members? Did various members clarify, summarize, interpret, support, initiate ideas, or conciliate?

(4) Did they give others a chance to talk, perhaps invite others to come into the discussion?

(5) Did members ask for evaluation during the session?

(6) Did members control irritability and were they able to absorb hostility?

(7) Did members show confidence in people?

(8) Could members phrase nondirective remarks accurately and well?

A Sample Post Meeting Reaction Sheet[3]

What did you think about this meeting? Please

be honest and objective. Your evaluation will help the leaders and the group improve the meetings.

1. How did you feel about the meeting? (check)

____

Poor Average Good Excellent

2. What do you think were the weaknesses?
3. What did you like about the meeting?
4. What changes or improvements would you suggest?

Do not sign your name.

1. Adapted from illustrations suggested by Jesse Ziegler in *International Journal of Religious Education* (May 1957).

2. Adapted from *My Group and I* by Gordon L. Lippitt and Warren H. Schmidt.

3. Adapted from *Dynamics of Participation Groups* by Gibb, Platts, and Miller, p. 46.

Chapter 10

Learning to Know and Be Known

Leadership is a function that is shared with members of a group. Mature persons strive for flexibility in leadership roles so that the needed leadership function may be contributed when needed. In performing leadership roles, persons become intimately involved with the Christian community; the leader recognizes that tensions among members waste valuable time, keep groups from performing necessary tasks, and if severe enough may make life in a group unbearable. On the other hand the leader knows that every group may improve its ways of working. It need not be bogged down with apathy or be torn by strife; people need not keep on talking past each other; the group can cultivate an atmosphere of acceptance and love where persons communicate with integrity and frankness.

The leader knows, too, that making the right decision may not be as important as paying attention to what is happening to people in the process; he sees all group meetings within the church as an opportunity to deepen Christian fellowship and build a sense of Christian community. He sees members of a group as persons with individual needs; he knows also that the Christian fellowship can help to meet these needs; he will pay attention to both maintenance and task roles. Christian leaders cannot assume that certain members have no worth-while contribution to make.

Growing in Sensitivity to the Needs of Others

Each member of a group is responsible for its growth. To help groups achieve this goal the individual member must grow himself. He must learn to look carefully for what is happening below the surface. He must become sensitive to the group needs of a given moment. He may have opportunity to help reduce the feelings of threat or insecurity of some persons in the group. It may seem a denial of the Christian spirit that persons belonging to church groups should feel threatened or insecure, but it happens. When relationships between persons in a group are pleasant, threat is reduced and the group is able to shift its attention from interpersonal problems to the task at hand.

Growing in Self-Insight

The way we perceive ourselves and others determines how we behave in groups. Numerous tests in laboratory groups show there may be a wide gap in the way an individual sees himself and how the group sees him. Our reactions in a group will be influenced by the way we *feel* we are accepted by the group and by the way the *group responds* to our attempts to influence it. The individual also responds to the way the group sees him, and will try to assume a role consistent with the group's perception. Herein lies a key for the group's redemptive action to help persons with needs.

In group relationships we find it difficult to be understood and find it equally hard to understand others. Perhaps the following quotation will make this clearer: "Two factors influence every interpersonal relationship. Both the way an individual *sees* the relationship and the way he *thinks* the other sees it will influence his actions. Each individual thinks that his own actions will be taken at face value, regardless of the underlying tensions or ambivalence he may feel. Also he makes continual guesses and inferences from the actions of other persons as to the other's actual attitudes and reactions. Our social codes require that we use our intuitive judgment in these guesses, since only among primitive societies and children are complete frankness and candid comment possible. Our actions may be interpreted very differently from what we intended and our guesses likewise may be erroneous. Both convention and personal sensitivity bar disclosure of our genuine attitudes in the majority of interpersonal situations. Direct comments regarding our attitudes seldom received genuine encouragement. The result is a great deal of sparring and hedging among people, even though they may desire deeper understanding and an honest basis of friendship. However, if one is involved in a situation, willingness to look at one's actions objectively is subject to the crossing of many emotional barriers. Self-analysis is complicated by our needs to preserve our self-esteem, and analysis of an interpersonal relationship is complicated by our previous social experiences. Frankness is complicated by our need for social approval, our needs to be friendly, pleasant, and well liked. True understanding and candid facing of attitudes and differences can only be achieved when both parties or, in the case of a group, all the parties have the same sincere desire to establish accurate interpersonal perceptions. Both productivity and harmony are in a large measure dependent upon the degree to which adjustments can be made to accurate perceptions of others."[1]

Learning to Use Feedback

One of the results of this study should be growth in understanding oneself and increased feeling for the needs of others. A powerful stimulant to personal growth in these areas is the proper use of feedback. Feedback is an expression borrowed from the field of electricity. The furnaces in homes today are wired to a feedback mechanism called a thermostat. When the temperature drops below 70 degrees, the mechanism sends an impulse that turns on the furnace. When the right temperature is reached, it turns off the furnace. Groups need feedback mechanisms to help them steer their course or to evaluate their progress. Individuals, too, constantly get feedback if they are sensitive enough to recognize it—of course, when someone "blows his stack," they can't miss getting it! Groups not only need a way of getting continuous self-correction, they also need to learn to grow and improve. Being able to collect adequate information about group process and to use it properly to make changes is a vital group function.

Occasionally, as pointed out in the previous session, the group may appoint an observer who gives the group feedback on its performance. Because feedback may take the form of criticism (often it is just that) we may not want to hear it. We have highly developed techniques for shrugging off criticism or we find ways to rationalize our behavior. Either we may take a sour grapes attitude toward the group, or try to live in a logic tight compartment. We can withdraw. This may be done by refusing to talk any more, by walking out of the meeting, quitting the group, or it may take the form of lack of interest, doodling, or side remarks.

Leaders who want to grow in interpersonal relationships become alert to feedback and use it wherever possible to help the group function more smoothly, and if the feedback is directed to their own ineptness in group relations they use it for self-improvement. We must learn to look at a group with sharper eyes in order to become aware of the below the surface forces which become feedback on the group's or the individual's performance.

Feedback is given in many ways. When people keep looking at their watches, it's a sign they are bored or, to say the least, they wish the meeting were over. When a member speaks with emotion and a flushed face, it may be hostility, threat, or embarrassment. If people keep talking all around a point without really confronting it, it may be a sign that the group does not feel free to bring it out into the open. Projection of blame on others, the belittling of some members, scapegoating, unfair generalizations, negative comments about planners or officers are all significant.

Stimulation to Personal Growth

One of the rewards of fellowship in a Christian group is that the group becomes a kind of mirror in which our real self is reflected to us. More likely than not, it will be a painful process to receive this kind of feedback, but it can be exceedingly helpful. Our self-image needs the correction that other Christians can help give us. Could this be what Paul had in mind when he wrote to the Ephesians: "But speaking the truth in love, may grow up into him in all things" (Eph. 4:15)?

We have already pointed out that we learn most through meaningful relationships with other persons. The Christian community can help the individual in many ways. It can provide opportunity to grow in self-insight; it can help him to become more sensitive to the needs of others.

In the Christian community we become sensitive to the needs persons have for acceptance, the need to develop self-respect, to receive recognition, personal fulfillment, and growth. Persons want to know that they have something of value to contribute and that they are appreciated.

We do not really know each other when our masks are on (defenses and pretenses)—but there is difficulty and danger in self-disclosure. We can only communicate with each other when we say what we mean. Learning to do this with love and forbearance is no mean task, but it can be an illuminating learning experience.

But the Christian is an individual too. He needs to discipline his rights and desires. He also needs time to be alone for prayer and meditation so he can be the person God intended him to be in his relations to others. He may need to stand alone against the group, because majorities have been known to be wrong. The group owes every individual the freedom to express his honest convictions. It owes him the right to be his own creative self.

The Meaning of These Studies to Church Groups

What is the meaning of these studies for the Christian community? There is a danger that we may fail to make clear how "learning to lead" relates to our Christian responsibility. Are Christian leaders really better prepared because they have learned something about the forces which operate in groups?

Hopefully, these studies should force us to re-examine the concept of the church as a community. They should clarify the truth that the Christian life is not lived in isolation, but in community.

The writer had an opportunity to worship with recent converts to Christianity in Africa. Just how far we in the West have drifted from community and into institutionalism was dramatically emphasized in this African setting. The structure in which these African Christians gathered on a mountainside could hardly be called a building. It had bamboo walls and a grass roof. We sat on banana leaves. There were no chairs or benches. Except for a few Bibles and the songbook in the leader's hand, there were no printed materials. There was no paid staff, no equipment. Whatever organization they had did not appear on the surface.

There were no signs of institutionalism as we know it, but these African Christians did have community. They knew each other. They provided a kind of Christian fellowship where the atmosphere of concern, confession, and commitment was contagious. There was recognition of the fact that an individual's sin was not merely a sin against God, but also a wrong against the brotherhood. One new convert rose to his feet to confess that he had sacrificed to an idol during the week. He said that he was sorry he did it in a moment of weakness. By what he said it was apparent that he knew he hurt the community by his conduct.

Here was a small cluster of Christians from a pagan environment gathered together for fellowship. If one wants to understand the young churches in Africa and Asia, he should read the Book of Acts again. They do not have much in this world's goods, they know little of institutionalism, but there one can identify many practices that build Christian community.

It is easy for us to surrender to institutionalism, to mistake it for the true church. Imposing edifices may hide the poverty of the Christian fellowship. Adequate space for classrooms and good equipment will not guarantee a truly Christian community. Large numbers of persons coming together for worship in one place, not knowing who is sitting in the next pew, hardly describes the New Testament concept of fellowship! Our Protestant background has also tended to accent individualism. Extreme emphasis on individualism makes the church a superficial doctrine, if we accept the view that the church is a *fellowship of believers*. We must pay more attention to removing the obstacles to Christian fellowship. We must help our groups to meet individual needs for belonging, acceptance, self-respect, self-confidence, recognition, fulfillment, and growth.

The Christian faith is intensely personal. No one can be a Christian on an impersonal basis. The Christian life begins with a personal, saving relationship to Jesus Christ. Furthermore, our full response to Christ's claim upon us involves us in His divine-human community. The fifteenth chapter of John describes this relationship. There the church is pictured as a vine. Not Christ alone, nor the believers alone. They are one. "I'm the vine, ye are the branches" (John 15:5).

Christians need each other. In the church groups to which we are related is found our opportunity to build and strengthen the quality of Christian fellowship.

1. Gibb, Platts, and Miller, *Dynamics of Participation Groups,* p. 10.

Why dont everyone stay
Class not properly divided
Physical conditions
Lack of ~~Interest~~
Goals
Class have different objection
discussion period
participation
discussion or lecture (age)

Problems in all groups
Student to study.